If you're reading this book, it isn't by accident. Your angels led you here. Let them continue to guide you forward!

I'm SOUL excited for your spiritual journey! Thank you for letting me be a part of it.

Sending You PEACE, BLISS and many blessings.

LOVE,

Julie and your Angels

2-IN-1 BOOK AND WORKBOOK

Angels and Awakening

JULIE JANCIUS
The Angel Medium™

A GUIDE TO RAISE YOUR VIBRATION AND HEAR YOUR ANGELS

ISBN 978-1-956996-00-5 (paperback), 978-1-956996-01-2 (hardback), 978-1-956996-02-9 (epub)

Published by:
Angel Wellness Center
A Division of Grow NPO, LLC
PO Box 5053, Wheaton, Illinois 60189
www.theangelmedium.com

Distributed in North America by: IngramSpark / Angel Wellness Center
Cover Design: Coversbyviolet.com
Publishing and Design Services: MartinPublishingServices.com
Editor: Sasha Banks
Photographer: Amanda Turner

DISCLAIMER TO MY READERS

This book is designed to provide information and motivation to its readers, with the understanding that the author does not intend to render any type of psychological, medical, mental, emotional, legal, religious or any other kind of professional advice, nor prescribe the use of any technique or practice as a form of treatment. Neither the publisher nor author shall be liable for any physical, psychological, emotional, spiritual, financial or commercial damages, including, but not limited to, special, incidental, consequential or other damages. The author, publisher and any other associate parties assume no responsibility for your actions and their consequences accrued from the advice and strategies in this book.

Always consult your physician or therapist when considering using meditation techniques. Always make sure to practice meditation in an environment that is safe. Do not engage in meditation activities while driving a car or operating any kind of machinery.

This book includes discussion on suicidal ideation. While the author has taken great lengths to ensure the subject matter is dealt with in a compassionate and respectful manner, it may be troubling for some readers and discretion is advised. If you are considering suicide or have a plan to take your life, please call the National Suicide Prevention Lifeline at 1-800-273-8255, or 911.

When You Sign Up For My

ANGEL MEMBERSHIP PROGRAM

You Have Access To:
A Year With Your Angels

A 12-Month Online Course Experience

You don't have to walk through your spiritual awakening alone.
Experience this program with a community of like-minded souls in my Angel Membership!

When my dad passed away and I started hearing from him before I even knew he was gone—I thought I was going crazy. I looked everywhere to find the answers I was seeking but none of those answers were in one spot. It took me years to piece it all together by connecting with my angels.

Friend, I didn't want you to struggle the way I did, so I created a year-long program for you with twelve online courses called *A Year With Your Angels*. It includes everything I've learned about angels and awakening over the years. In it you'll walk through every step of your spiritual awakening and gain a greater understanding of your soul, purpose and angels.

When you sign up for my Angel Membership, you'll have access to my A Year With Your Angels Program (one month at a time). You'll also have access to

1. Small groups;
2. Live group meetings/sacred events with me each month where you can ask me questions; and
3. A private online community where you can connect with hundreds of like-minded souls who are awakening too!

This book was written to go along with the first three courses in my **_A Year With Your Angels Program_**. Here's what people are saying about the book and program:

> "Julie has literally changed the vibration of my life and made me feel like a part of her angel family. She swears, she cries, she feels, she believes, and she cares! Thank you, Julie, for sharing your gifts, training, and insights with us. Your words have had a tremendous impact on my life and the lives of my friends and family. This book and your teachings are gifts that I will treasure and continue to learn from."
>
> —Stephanie Moyes, Angel Member

> "Julie's teachings have helped my life immensely. Since signing up for the Angel Membership, I have learned to evolve so much spiritually and emotionally. It has helped me to understand my emotions, work through triggers, and learn how to take control of my own energy, bringing calm and peace to my life. I continue to grow and make major positive life changes. Now that I have also taken the Angel Reiki School, I hope to help others as well."
>
> —Lisa Wetherbee, Angel Member

Your Spirit Team says that you've read all the books, you've listened to all the podcasts, you've been seeking for so long—this is the year you put it all together to live the joyous life your soul was born to live! My Angel Membership program is the resource you've been searching for. Register today at www.theangelmedium.com and I look forward to working with you!

WWW.THEANGELMEDIUM.COM

Win A
FREE ANGEL READING
with Julie!

Julie is always giving out freebies to people who've purchased this book and subscribed to her email list! It's as easy as 1, 2, 3:

1. Head over to www.theangelmedium.com

2. Go to the menu and click "books"

3. Scroll down and subscribe to Julie's email list

You must stay subscribed to the email list to win! Check your email for a new winner each month. As part of Julie's email list you'll receive a new message from your angels each week!

WWW.THEANGELMEDIUM.COM

DEDICATION

Thank you God for entrusting me to do Your work—all of the glory goes to You.

For Blake and Elle, whose unconditional love and encouragement has allowed me to live the fullest expression of my soul. Living this lifetime with you is the greatest gift. For my mom who taught me how to follow my heart and built me up with words of faith. For my dad who wouldn't let death keep us apart. And for my teams (Spirit Team and Earth-Bound Spirit Team) who make it all come together. None of this would be possible without you.

This book is dedicated to you, beautiful soul. If you're here to do your spiritual work, be proud of yourself and know this is evidence that your angels are already working with you!

CONTENTS

*To get to know your angels on the deepest level, please move through this book slowly
over the course of twelve weeks (as laid out for you below).*

Week Three

Week Four

ANGEL COMMUNICATION

Part 1

Week One

Week Two

Week Three

Week Four

ANGEL COMMUNICATION

INTRODUCTION
How I Started Hearing From Heaven

In August 2015, I started hearing from my deceased, estranged father a month before I was informed of his passing. Unbeknownst to me, he was communicating with me by flooding my imagination with memories of my childhood, helping me to feel his presence, and hearing him speak to me through my own internal dialogue (intuition).

Starting the day my dad passed, everytime I would brush my daughter's hair I would hear, "She needs a hair brush like I used." A month later, I was in a work meeting when my sister phoned me several times in a row. As soon as she spoke the words, "He's gone," I saw a vision within my imagination of my dad combing my hair before school (as he always did) with his hair brush, which I hadn't thought about in over 25 years.

My dad always used a wooden-handle, boar-bristle hair brush and it dawned on me! I knew my dad had been the one saying, "She needs a hair brush like I used," because my daughter has his hair and he was right. She did indeed need a brush like his to work through the tangles!

While there was a deep love and bond between me and my dad, we didn't agree on very much in this life and it tore us apart. But what so deeply shook me to my core was that even on the Other Side, my dad's love for me softened the anger I'd felt toward him and would not allow his death to separate us. Right now, your loved ones in Heaven are whispering in your ear, "Same goes for you too. We're not gone, we're right next to you. You just have to learn *how* to communicate with us so that you feel us more in your everyday life!"

Friend, my life's work is teaching you to make this connection for yourself! After working with my angels for years and studying with world-renowned healers, I started the top-charted spiritual podcast (also called Angels and Awakening) and online courses so that I could share everything I learned with you!

With every ounce of my being, this is what I know for sure: you have a Spirit Team made up of angels, loved ones, and guides on the Other Side—every soul does! On my journey, I realized Spirit had been talking to me my whole life, I just never understood how. I didn't know their language back then, but I do now. My purpose is to teach you the language of the angels so that you understand how they're personally leading you, in your everyday life.

While I believe you will come away from this book with a wealth of information, insight, and practices, I have more tools available for those who'd like to go deeper! This book corresponds with three courses in my Angel Membership program called *Oneness, Angel Communication Part 1,* and *Angel Communication Part 2,* which I invite you to join!

You can a) Purchase these courses separately on the website www.theangelmedium.com or b) Join the Angel Membership program for access to my *A Year With Your Angels Program* that leads you through twelve online courses (one month at a time) and includes small groups, live group access to me each month, teaching videos, meditations, energy healing recordings, and so much more!

When you invest in my Angel Membership you'll create daily spiritual practices that strengthen your ability to: align with the energy of the Other Side; connect with your angels; know your Spirit team; trust your intuition; find your purpose; remove energetic blockages; rewrite your story; rewire your mind; work with your angels on ancestral trauma and inner child work; protect yourself as a highly-sensitive empath; and build a relationship with your own loved ones on the Other Side.

As the founder of Angel Reiki, I also have a separate certificate program, Angel Reiki School, for people who want to develop their unique God-given gifts, start a spiritual business, work one-on-one with others and help raise the vibration of the planet.

Friend, I'm *SOUL* excited for you to dive in, but before you do there are a few more things to know. There is no ghosty vibe, when you hear from the Other Side; that's all a myth. Your Spirit Team is a gift given to you by God to help you navigate this beautiful life. When you connect with the Other Side, it feels like standing in God's presence. I call this energy Oneness; it is the energy of God. God's energy is the highest vibrational frequency, radiating love, joy, peace, bliss, ease, and grace. To connect with the Other Side and follow the divine wisdom of your soul is to follow God's will and allow God to lead your life.

With this book, you are taking the first step in connecting with the Other Side to hear your own messages. Again, this book is written in two parts that correspond with the Angel Membership program. *Oneness* is the first part of this book, and is one month long. My books and courses are not meant to be read or perfected in one sitting; they were channeled for you to walk slowly through the pages, deeply and fully immerse yourself in the exercises, and allow Spirit to open your consciousness to a miraculous world that has alway been in front of you, but that you never knew existed (or how to access).

We begin with the *Oneness* portion of the book because without it, true communication with the Other Side is simply not possible. Oneness is like a radio that helps you dial into the frequency and messages of your Spirit Team. Once you know how to feel and hold Oneness, you're ready to connect with your angels.

The second part of this book is *Angel Communication,* which is two months long. You'll spend a few days getting to know who each angel is, their role in your life, and the signs they show you to validate their presence. At the end of the book, you'll know exactly who is on your Spirit Team and I'll even give you a quick lesson on connecting with your loved ones in Heaven to hear their personal messages for you.

Consultants suggested I split this book into two: a separate book and workbook, but I didn't want you to have to purchase an additional guide, so here it is for you (a full book and a full workbook) all combined into one. It is my hope that you enjoy this incredible soul-discovery journey. Don't forget to register your email and receipt on my website for special freebies!

As you read this book, please don't let terminology stop you from learning! Friend, I was raised in a Catholic school, wanting to be a priest and then a nun (when I learned females cannot be priests). As a result, I use the term "God" in my work, but please feel free to replace it with Universe, Source, Spirit, I Am, All That Is, or any name that resonates most with you. "God" is a man-made term. The only name God actually uses to refer to Themself is "Yahweh," in Exodus 3:14 (which translates to "I am who I am"). So truly, any name you use to refer to God works! One final note: because God is genderless, you'll see me use They, Them, Their pronouns.

Friend, your angels and loved ones on the Other Side surround you right here, right now. Our prayer for you is that by the end of this book, you feel the infinite magnitude of how special you are in the eyes of God; you know who is on your Spirit Team and the signs they send you; and you are able to create your own Heaven on Earth with your Spirit Team by your side. I'm *SOUL* excited for you, now let's dive in!

ONENESS

Raise Your Vibration

ONENESS

Week One

Practice the Oneness Meditation

for three minutes every day for one month. Practice one minute when you wake up, one minute at lunch, and one minute before bed by repeating the meditation to yourself.

If you're in the Angel Membership,

go to the Oneness course:

☐ Watch **Teaching Video One**.

☐ Watch the Oneness Meditation video.

☐ Participate in your choice of any small group and live events this month.

HEAVEN ON EARTH
Through Awakening

This life is not what you think it is and you are not who you think you are. You are so much more! And if you are reading this book, you are awakening.

When I woke up, I was at a breaking point in my life. I was desperately trying to please everyone: my husband, my boss, my mom. I wanted to be a good wife and mom, and a good employee. Somewhere along my life journey, I equated being good and successful with fitting in and being who others wanted me to be, in order to be *liked*.

In my attempt to please everyone else, I lost myself. I loved my husband, but we didn't know how to communicate and our marriage was a mess. I loved my work, but my boss and I did not "click." I worked overtime around the clock, for months to please her, spending little to no time with my daughter. My efforts did not pay off at work, and I felt like a terrible mom and wife at home. I felt like a failure in every area of my life and my spirit, the part of me that was passionate and excited about life, broke.

There is a saying, "Spirit will shake you to awaken you." That couldn't be more true!

The angels say each soul takes a different path to arrive at their spiritual awakening journey. While some proactively work to awaken with ease, many souls are thrust into a journey of awakening through challenging times in their life. Perhaps you can relate: the loss of a loved one, not feeling like you fit in, an unhealthy relationship, an illness, losing a job, not understanding your purpose. The angels can take any situation in your life and use it to lead you back to God and to yourself, and that is exactly what awakening is—journeying back to self.

I'm not talking about your human self, I'm talking about a journey back to your soul self.

There are many phases of awakening, but it all begins with Oneness. Oneness is a rebirth that affirms who you are as a soul, your oneness with God, the ways your soul is made up of God's energy, and how the voice of your soul lives within you as your intuition. Through this remembrance of self, you can step back into union with God and begin to live each day in God's energy, with which you can rebuild your life and create your own Heaven on Earth.

This time, as you build the life your soul came here to live, you're not going to build it by society's standards. To awaken and rebuild means co-creating your life hand-in-hand with God. Friend, I know you want this process to be a quick one. However, just as it takes nine months for a human baby to become fully developed in the womb, creating a life you love takes time and tools.

The miracle is, God gave us tools to both stay connected to Their energy and rebuild our lives to be magical, miraculous, and like Heaven on Earth: those tools are angels. Angels are extensions of God's energy, and just as each soul on Earth has a specific purpose, every angel has a role, responsibilities, and a purpose.

Imagine God gave every soul on Earth all the tools needed to build their own house. God provided the wood, cement, windows, roofing, power tools, plumbing tools, electrical tools, etc. However, if you don't know the difference between a plumbing tool and an electrical tool, they're both useless to you because you don't know how to use them—same when it comes to your angels.

Friend, you have big, deep purpose in this lifetime. It is no accident that your soul is here, right now, at one of the most pivotal moments on Earth. Your angels know your purpose and they know you deeply. You have Cherubim angels, Seraphim angels, Archangels, guardian angels, angel guides, and loved ones on the Other Side working on your behalf every moment of every day. Because you do not know who they are, you cannot yet use the tools they possess to help you better your life.

Your job is to get to know your angels. (Let me say that again because it is so vitally important): Your job is to get to know your angels. You have angels beside you to help you heal past emotional pain, find your joy, speak your truth, fine-tune your intuition, and step into the role God gave you. When you can call on them each by name, they become friends who support you in your everyday life.

When you understand how all of your angels are working with you, you'll develop a relationship with them and communicating with them will become easy. You can't communicate well with someone you don't know, which is why simply getting to know your angels changes everything! When you know them, you see them show up in your life every day and feel their presence. You become familiar with their voice and, over time, you begin to experience hearing them whisper in your ear, showing you visions through your imagination, and providing you with clear knowingness.

Learning to hold the vibration of Oneness and getting to know your angels are the first two steps in your spiritual awakening journey.

Oneness is like a radio that allows you to connect with the Other Side. It is the tool you need before any other communication can occur. And getting to know your angels is like fiddling with the radio station dial until you hear the Other Side clearly. It is the tool you need to know which station they're coming through the most clearly. This book gifts you with both of these tools.

To awaken is to gain your life back, and that's what I want for you! It's why you're here and it's what this book and the Angel Membership program are all about.

Let's begin with Oneness—the biggest tool of all. Oneness creates and strengthens an impenetrable connection with God, your angels, and your loved ones on the Other Side in order to establish the unshakable faith of who you are and the courage you need to take your next step.

YOU ARE ONE WITH ALL THAT IS

Friend, understand that you are one with All That Is. Have you ever had a challenging time in your life when you thought to yourself, "I wish I knew the answer?" You do! Your soul is connected to the divine wisdom of All That Is, of I Am, of God. When you learn to connect to God-energy, it does not matter where you go in life or what happens, because you are able to connect to God, pray, ask questions and hear positive, loving answers within your heart.

Your soul is one droplet in the ocean that is God that can never be separate from the rest of the ocean. Your soul can never be separate from God. In fact, you are not separate from any other life here on Earth because you are one with every living and non-living thing! More than that, you are one with everything everywhere.

Stop to consider this: as one droplet in the ocean that is God which can never be separated from the ocean, you are every soul walking this Earth and every soul walking this Earth is you. Understanding this, means you understand that to hurt another, is to hurt yourself.

When everyone on Earth understands their Oneness, life on Earth will be transformed and become a heavenly place of peace.

God's gift to you is your freewill, your choice. You do not have to wait for all other souls in humanity to awaken. You get to live in Heaven on Earth starting now, and as you hold that vibration of "Heaven on Earth," of Oneness, you become part of a collective that is holding the same energy and vision. Holding the vibration of Oneness not only raises the vibration here on Earth, but works to shift each individual mind, one at a time, to become one as well.

WHAT IS ONENESS?

When we experience "Heaven" or the Other Side, there is an energy specific to that realm. The energy of Heaven is the state of Oneness and divine union with God. It is an energy of love, joy, peace, bliss, ease and grace, but we don't have to pass away to feel it. You do not have to go through dramatic and hard times in your life to feel it. It is your birthright to live in the energy of Oneness with God, now and always.

Remember, your soul is one with All That Is. It means this energy can never be taken away from you and cannot leave you: Oneness is you.

People call the state of Oneness many things. For a long time I called it "high vibration," but I've found that the word "high" creates a hierarchy of energy that implies a binary, whereas the word "Oneness" does not. Others call it "the now," "presence," "bliss," "nirvana," "enlightenment" and so on.

Many people search, study, and travel the world for decades looking for this particular state of being. Others try to find a state of Oneness by filling a void within themselves. They do this by attaining someone or something: the biggest house, the most expensive car, the most attractive spouse, the best body, or even agelessness.

The lie the world has told you is that you need something outside of you to be whole, but you do not. There is nothing you can buy, do, say, or achieve to become one with God.

You are one with the whole and the only way to Oneness is going within yourself, feeling the energy within your body, and learning to feel energy and vibrational frequency itself. Philosophers and thinkers have contemplated the words to describe the energy of Oneness for millenia. Truthfully, no word exists to describe it and that is because Oneness cannot be intellectualized. Oneness (God's energy) is palpable and must be felt.

HOW DO YOU GET INTO A STATE OF ONENESS?

There are many different ways to experience Oneness. Some people call them portals to experiencing the divine. I will guide you through the Oneness Meditation, helping you open your crown chakra. You'll bring the energy of Oneness through the crown of the head, into the heart, and you will start to feel that your heart is one with your body; your heart and body are one with the air surrounding you; your heart, body and the air surrounding you are one with all life here on Earth, and everything, everywhere.

"Why the crown chakra?" Remember back to seeing a photo of Jesus with the gold circle behind his head. This is not just found in Christian paintings, but in paintings of spiritual figures from Eastern culture, Ancient Greece, Ancient Rome, Hinduism, Islam, and Buddhism. What does it represent? Some say this is a "halo" signifying the subject was a spiritual leader; however, Spirit says it represents unity and Oneness with the Other Side. When you learn energy healing, the energy of each chakra feels completely different and holds different information. The crown chakra holds the energy of connection with God, and the ancients knew this, especially the painters who were in Oneness and felt this energy as they painted.

People misunderstand Oneness when they bring the energy to the crown of their head and stop there. Feeling this energy in the crown is wonderful, but to feel Oneness we must pull the energy into our hearts. From there, we can feel our Oneness with All That Is in an expansive way that is felt with the entire being. The crown chakra is not Oneness itself. You must *embody* Oneness. The crown chakra is just one portal to the energy of All That Is. To feel Oneness you have to go deeper.

ONENESS MEDITATION

It is best to pause here and play the "Oneness Meditation" audio recording in the Angel Membership, Oneness Course (look in the folder named *A Year With Your Angels*). You can listen to my voice guide you throughout this meditation as many times as you need until you can walk yourself through it by saying the words to yourself within your mind. Once you can walk yourself through the meditation, create a routine for one minute, three times a day to practice getting into a state of Oneness.

If you are not part of the Angel Membership, see the words to the meditation below. You can read this and feel the energy or have someone else read this to you as you get into Oneness. The same principle applies here: practice until you can say the words to yourself within your mind. Once you've got it, practice getting into Oneness for one minute, three times a day.

ONENESS MEDITATION

Close your eyes and begin by taking a deep breath in.
Breath out and lengthen your breath so the exhale extends longer than the inhale.

I want you to imagine that your socks and shoes are off.
Your bare feet connect with the soil of the Earth.

Down through the bottoms, the soles of your feet,
are large roots that go down far and wide into the Earth.
These roots anchor you to the Earth as if you were a tree.
These roots ground you.

Up through these roots comes a yummy,
tingly energy that you begin to feel at the tips of your toes.
Allow that yummy, tingly energy to move up your feet and around your ankles.
(*Pause and take a deep breath in, deep breath out.)

Feel this sparkly energy move up your calves and shins,
all the way up to your knees.
(*Pause and take a deep breath in, deep breath out.)

Feel this yummy, tingly energy move up your thighs and hamstrings,
all the way up to the sides of your hips.
(*Pause and take a deep breath in, deep breath out.)

Once you feel this yummy, tingly energy at the sides of your hips,
allow it to move up to the base of your spine and stomach.
Feel this yummy energy as it dances up your spine and stomach,
all the way up until it reaches your heart.
(*Pause and take a deep breath in, deep breath out.)

Feel how this yummy energy fills your entire heart,
and surrounds your entire heart.
And as it does, it gently brings your body into a state of ease.
(*Pause and take a deep breath in, deep breath out.)

Allow this beautiful, loving energy to rise into your shoulders, into your neck.
And feel it as it fills your entire head front to back, side to side, top to bottom.
(*Pause and take a deep breath in, deep breath out.)

Allow this tingly energy to move through the hair follicles on the top of your head.

To where you now feel this yummy, tingly energy above the top of your head.

This energy above your head may feel airy or floaty.

It might feel spacious and expansive.

The energy above your head might feel as though you have a string connected to the crown of your head, and it's pulling you upwards towards the sky.

Just notice what it is you feel.

(*Pause and take a deep breath in, deep breath out.)

Now imagine there is an opening at the crown of your head.

This opening is the size of a soup bowl at the top of your head.

Imagine that God's love and God's energy begins to pour down,

like a gentle waterfall, in through the crown of your head.

God's energy moves through your head, down to your heart,

and it begins to pool and surround your heart.

(*Pause and take a deep breath in, deep breath out.)

I want you to notice your breath.

Notice how your physical heart is one with your body.

(*Pause and take a deep breath in, deep breath out.)

Notice how your heart and body are one with the air surrounding you.

(*Pause and take a deep breath in, deep breath out.)

Notice how your heart, body and air surrounding you are one with all plant life here on earth.

(*Pause and take a deep breath in, deep breath out.)

Notice how your heart, body and air surrounding you are one with all animal life here on earth.

(*Pause and take a deep breath in, deep breath out.)

Notice how your heart, body and air surrounding you are one with all people here on earth,

and with all things everywhere throughout the multiverse and the Other Side.

(*Pause and take a deep breath in, deep breath out.)

Feel how you are one with All That Is.

(*Pause and take a deep breath in, deep breath out.)

EXPERIENCING ONENESS

Over the next four weeks, you will learn to feel and hold the vibration of Oneness. Can you learn all this in four weeks? Absolutely yes, you can! You must have faith and believe! Below is an overview of the steps you will follow each week:

Week One: Practice the Oneness Meditation for three minutes every day for one month: one minute when you wake up, one minute at lunch, one minute before bed by repeating the meditation to yourself. This might take you more time at the beginning but as you keep practicing you will get into Oneness energy more quickly.

Week Two: Find blocks of time throughout your week when you're doing a mindless activity. Make it a routine to practice holding Oneness during these times in order to expand the length of time you're in Oneness throughout your day.

Week Three: Practice holding Oneness during conversations.

Week Four: Practice holding Oneness while doing. Discover that there isn't any moment where you are separate from All That Is. Every moment of doing, thinking, talking, speaking, being—you are one with All That Is.

WHAT DOES ONENESS FEEL LIKE?

When you practice the Oneness Meditation, you may first notice that you feel tingly energy above the top of your head, neck, and shoulders. Some have described feeling as though a string is attached to the crown of their head, lifting them upwards towards the sky. Some have described a spacious feeling of expansiveness above them; when you feel this, it is just the first step.

Take this energy from above the head, imagine an opening in the crown of your head, and allow this yummy energy to go in through the top of your head. As you feel this yummy tingly energy come through the top of your head, notice that it pools in and around your heart. Next, focus your attention on:

1. Your heart being one with your body

2. Your heart and body being one with the air surrounding you

3. Your heart, body and the air surrounding you being one with all life here on Earth

4. Feel Oneness with everything on Earth and everything, everywhere

When you follow these steps, you will begin to feel a state of expansion. Your awareness is no longer isolated to the body, as has been your set point of being for most of your life. Instead, when you are in Oneness, your energy cannot be confined to the body. You are connected to the life force of everything, everywhere in this life and beyond.

When you sit in a state of Oneness, and relax into the elements of Oneness, there is simply love, joy, peace, bliss, ease, and grace. The love you feel is so beautiful it may make you want to cry, as you've likely not known love to that degree in this lifetime. The sense of joy and bliss are more than happiness. Those sensations are a remembrance of your natural state of euphoria and all the beauty that surrounds you in every area of your life, right here in the now. You remember that while happiness is fleeting, joy and bliss can never leave you. Joy and bliss are with you always. The sense of peace is grand like the depth of the ocean and you become aware that you are always divinely protected, guarded, and guided.

Find peace and comfort knowing that this energy force holds within it every energy and every answer you will ever need in this lifetime.

PORTALS TO ONENESS

There are many portals to experiencing Oneness. The word "portal" sounds "woo woo," but I assure you it is not. Portals are simply openings between you and the Other Side, which you can use to connect with God's energy. All of the following are portals to this energy:

Angels

Prayer

The Rosary

The Crown Chakra

Silence

Stillness

Meditation

Deep Breathing

The Heart Chakra

Reiki and Other Energy
    Healing/Clearing Modalities

Servitude

Compassion

Being Near Water

Crystals

Being Present

Essential Oils

Being in Nature

Each of these contains the elements of silence, stillness, release of thought, focus on no-thought, and letting go—a total surrender. Make space for Oneness in your life by turning off the noise around you and simply focusing on your breath. Do this as often as possible! In the first year I learned to hold Oneness, I kept the TV and radio turned off much of the time. Every chance I got to sit still in silence and practice holding the energy was a beautiful opportunity. Do the same for yourself!

TELL YOURSELF, "THIS IS EASY! I DID IT!"

In Disney's movie "Soul," Dorothea Williams tells Joe Gardner this story:

"I heard this story about a fish, he swims up to an older fish and says: 'I'm trying to find this thing they call the ocean.'"

"'The ocean?' the older fish says, 'That's what you're in right now.'"

"'This?' says the young fish, 'This is water. What I want is the ocean!'"

The moral of the story is this: Oneness is here now, right in front of you. It surrounds you, and is within you. Deeper than that, it *is* you and you are it.

You are Oneness. You are connected to the Oneness of All That Is.

You might think, "Julie, that's just air." No. You're trying to find Oneness and you're in Oneness right now. The divinity of God surrounds you, wraps you, and moves through you.

WHY ONENESS IS SO IMPORTANT

Oneness makes connecting with the Other Side, your Angels, and loved ones easier. After just one month of learning about Oneness, you will have the foundation to all other work you do spiritually. Think about it like this: you're in the car, you turn the radio to your favorite station and hear the DJ's voice clearly. But when you turn the dial one notch to the left or right, you no longer hear clearly. That one small step means now all you hear is static, "Schhhhhhhhhhhhhhh."

This is an analogy for your spiritual health and spiritual work. When you learn to hold Oneness, you're really learning to get into alignment with the right radio frequency to hear the Other Side more clearly. Without this work, you will wade through years of spiritual work trying to learn how to tap into your intuition, learn energy work, and how to connect with your angels all with the radio dial set to the wrong channel! Imagine trying to do all that work while hearing static. You may approach a spiritual teacher and say, "I can't hear!"

They might ask, "Are you in Oneness?"

"No," you say.

"Why not?"

"I didn't think it was a big deal."

We begin all spiritual work with Oneness because it is the opening. Oneness is the way. Oneness is your soul's vibration—it is everything. Without Oneness as your foundation, you will struggle more than you need to.

KEEP IT POSITIVE FOR ONE MONTH

I have found that when teaching students how to get into and hold the space of Oneness, it is difficult for them to both work through past pain or try to solve the big problems of the world within their minds, and learn to hold Oneness at the same time. Oneness is union, harmony, and singularity. The opposite of Oneness is duality: Me vs. you; us vs. them; I'm here, you're there; they're bad, I'm good; etc. To make learning how to hold Oneness easier for you, I'm asking you to set aside for one month:

- ⌘ All judgements of yourself and others
- ⌘ Negative thinking about yourself and others
- ⌘ Gossip
- ⌘ Politics
- ⌘ Thoughts of past emotional pain or triggers
- ⌘ Trying to figure out how to be a "nice, good" person while also holding Oneness at the same time.

You may say, "But Julie, I want to understand how those topics tie into my spirituality." There are many dynamics and complexities to divine knowledge. While we don't have enough room in this book to cover them, over the course of the first year of the Angel Membership, we closely dissect low vibrations, negative thoughts, and pain energy. But first, you must learn Oneness or the rest will not make sense.

For one month, please keep everything focused on Oneness in your personal life, your thoughts, your spoken and written words, and here while reading this book. Be the observer of your thoughts.

AM I NOT SUPPOSED TO THINK?

What is thought? Your soul has two components. Your soul is energy that vibrates and your soul has thought consciousness or intuition. Your body has two components. Your body is energy that vibrates and your body has an additional thought system which is the Egoic Mind; this means you have two thought systems within yourself—Egoic Mind and intuition. You only have an Egoic Mind while here on Earth; it is a living energy within the head that is tied to your DNA, and holds a record of everything your ancestors have experienced. The Egoic Mind has kept you and your family alive through fear for millennia. Your family line has survived the caveman era, plagues, wars, and more by listening to that fear voice within. This fear voice produces a physical response within your body of anxiety, stress, tension, shame, terror or other low vibrational frequencies. Truthfully, the Egoic Mind has served humanity well until now. We are now living in a time where many no longer have to fear attacks by animals or where their next meal is going to come from; however, the Egoic Mind hasn't gotten the memo and has taken over most minds within humanity. Most humans now believe they are their thoughts, leading them to follow their thoughts blindly. Humans are no longer in control of what they are thinking because their thoughts control them, which is a huge problem given that humanity bases their daily actions and reactions on subconscious thinking.

From the moment you wake up in the morning until the moment you go to sleep at night, your day is dominated by what your Egoic Mind wants you to think and do. Your thoughts produce feelings and emotions within you that cause you to act and react.

Awakening means coming out of this zombie-like Egoic Mind state and being mindful of your energy, thoughts, feelings, your reactions, words, and how you behave.

No human can get their Egoic Mind to go away completely, but everyone can learn to become the observer of their thoughts so that their Egoic Mind no longer controls them. When you observe your thoughts, it is your intuition (your Higher Self or God-consciousness) that is the observer: this is your soul's thought system, a higher form of thought.

You've heard people say, "Listen to your heart." If you did not have these two thought systems, the Egoic Mind and your intuition, people would just say, "Go think for a while." I've heard it said that scientists who have studied thought do not know where thought comes from, that it just flows to you.

If you have thoughts while practicing the Oneness Meditation, I want you to acknowledge that thought by observing it and letting it pass by. When you judge, believe, or attach to your thoughts, you create a "train of thought" that takes you where it wants to go; most times it is a state of division, separation, and duality. Instead of allowing your thoughts to run away with you, you can remain in a state of Oneness by allowing your thoughts to flow by like clouds passing in the sky.

If your thoughts persist, you may have to talk to them and then allow them to flow by. Here are a few examples:

Example of a Thought Spiral

You see a boy at the bus stop at the end of your street. The boy is in shorts, despite the fact that it's winter and there's snow on the ground. Seeing the boy in shorts bothers you. You think, "Why is he wearing shorts? Doesn't he know how cold it is? What if he gets sick? I should really tell him to put on long pants. Maybe I'll call his mother!"

What just happened here? You saw the boy and the judge within your head said, "Shorts! Why in the world is he wearing shorts?" From this initial thought, you have one of two options. You can see the thought, let it pass by and say, "Hi thought! I see you! I understand this upsets you, but we're not in charge of that boy, so we're not going to discuss it further." Doing this allows you to choose not to attach to the thought and not to let the thought control you.

When you attach to the thought you allow yourself to hop on the Negative Thought Express Train and that thought will spiral. When a thought spirals, the initial thought quickly becomes 10, 30, 50, or perhaps 100 new thoughts.

The initial thought is, "Shorts! Why in the world is he wearing shorts?" And when you attach to that singular thought, it quickly becomes a series of thoughts, "Doesn't he know how cold it is? How dumb. What a weirdo!" So not only have you attached to the thought and judged them, but you've now gone down a spiral that's led you to judging this random boy, who you know nothing about!

Thought spirals are not necessary. It is well within your control to let a thought spiral or not. It is within your control to be aware of a thought within your head and allow it to pass on by without attaching to it or allowing the thought to progress.

Example of Believing a Thought

We judge ourselves as much, if not more, than we judge others. A thought may arise within you about yourself, and if your initial reaction is to believe the thought, it too will become a train of thought that will run away and take you where it wants you to go. It works like this:

Initial Thought: "I'm heavier than I've ever been!"

Thought Spiral: "I shouldn't have eaten like that last night. I always do this to myself. I've never been able to get my weight under control. I want to lose weight, but I don't want to fail again. I always fail at this. Why am I so bad at this?"

When you believe the initial thought, the thought tends to spiral downward into negative and heavy energies. It can help to see your Egoic Mind as a child or your teenage self who does not know better. Instead of being frustrated with the thought itself, accept that you cannot stop the initial thoughts from coming in, but you can stop the spiral. Instead, try this when you have the initial thought:

> *Initial Thought:* "I'm heavier than I've ever been."

> *Oneness Response:* "My body is incredible and has always been reliable. My body has gotten me through some pretty major things in this lifetime, and I'm proud of it. I love my body. I'm grateful to my body!"

When you believe a thought, you anchor into it by saying, "Yes, this thought is correct. I am so bad. I've done this and that." This negative inward self-talk separates you from your Oneness with God, categorizing you as good or bad. You don't have to let it do this to you. You have power over your Egoic-Minded thoughts. You are the gatekeeper of thought and what you will and will not allow is fully up to you!

Be patient with yourself. All your life, you've been trained to think from your subconscious Egoic Mind. You have thought pathways within your mind that make it easy to spiral into judgment. You cannot expect to rewire your mind overnight. You absolutely must give yourself grace and be patient as you become more aware of your thoughts and teach yourself to live in a state of Oneness with less thought.

LIMIT YOUR DISTRACTIONS

It would be enough to simply concentrate on holding the energy of Oneness this month and becoming more aware of your thoughts, but we are programmed to consume large amounts of content outside of ourselves all day long. We turn on the TV, music, audio books, check the news, open our emails, social media, shop on the web and all of this impacts our ability to learn how to feel and hold Oneness; not all of this consumption is bad, but learning to hold the energy of Oneness requires your mindful attention because it doesn't take very long for you to become depleted energetically.

Let's say you start your day out with a full battery at 100% energy, but every time you check the news it drains your energy by 5%. Every time you check social media, it drains your energy by 5%. When you become overwhelmed after opening your email, it drains your energy by 5%.

For one month, refrain from as much outside distraction as possible. Instead, allow there to be more silence, stillness, and quiet in your life.

USE YOUR BREATH AS A PORTAL

Anytime you need to redirect your thoughts or keep your mind from wandering, bring your attention to your breath. Your breath is a portal to Oneness. Focus on breathing in and out through your nose and lengthening each inhale and exhale. While extending the inhale and exhale, you can either focus on:

⌘ Feeling your chest expand with each inhale and feeling the exhale release every ounce of breath within your body.

⌘ Or extending the breath by counting on the inhale and counting on the exhale. When counting, extend the breath by one count each time. If it takes you 5-seconds to inhale, aim for a six-second exhale. Then aim for a seven-second inhale and eight-second exhale. Extend your breath as much as you can so long as it still feels natural. Do not go beyond the limits of your body. I can get to about an 11-second inhale and 13-second exhale which feels natural and comfortable to me. Do what feels best for you!

Sometimes, I visualize God's energy being breathed into me through the crown of my head. That yummy energy comes down into my heart, filling it with God's love. I then exhale love up and out of the crown of my head. As I do, I feel the pulse of life and Oneness with All That Is. Friend, I want you to use these tools for yourself!

WHAT IF I DON'T HAVE TIME TO MEDITATE?

When it comes to meditation, there are two schools of thought: some believe that we must be seated, doing nothing but meditating. Others believe that we can tune our vibration to God's vibration and carry that energy with us throughout the day. I believe the latter. It's about living more deeply within a state of Oneness for much of your day, by bringing your mind and energy back to Oneness each time it wanders.

When I started doing this work, I was a busy mom with a career myself. I assumed that getting into a state of Oneness and learning to hold the energy would mean meditating for eight hours a day. This seemed daunting and I knew if that were true, I didn't have the time for it. But it was not true and every time I had that thought, I could see Spirit shaking their head "no."

I have lived and taught this for years, and I can tell you with certainty that while sitting in lotus position for eight hours a day may work for some people, it is not the only way to achieve the benefits of meditation. In the beginning, Spirit would say to me, "Spend three micro minutes with us every day, one minute when you first wake up, one minute at lunch, and one minute before you lay your head on your pillow at night."

Three minutes of meditation a day is all it takes to shift your life!

What ends up happening in those three minutes each day, is that you turn yourself to God's frequency of Oneness. You use the portals and the Oneness Meditation until one day, you are going about your day, minding your own business and you find yourself in a state of Oneness without even trying. I get emails from people all the time when they achieve this!

Now it's time for you to practice the Oneness Meditation for one minute, three times a day as you repeat the steps in your mind. One day you'll wake up and say, "I want to feel Oneness." And it will be there! You'll be in it and able to go about your day carrying Oneness.

Record your progress! Tell me what Oneness feels like to you.

_____

_____

_____

_____

_____

_____

_____

_____

_____

_____

_____

_____

_____

_____

_____

_____

_____

_____

_____

_____

ONENESS
Week Two

Continue practicing the Oneness Meditation

for three minutes every day: One minute when you wake up, one minute at lunch, and one minute before bed.

Notice blocks of time throughout your week when you're engaged in a mindless activity. Make it a routine to practice holding Oneness during these times in order to expand the length of time you're in Oneness throughout your day.

If you're in the Angel Membership,

go to the Oneness course (in the folder titled *A Year With Your Angels*):

☐ Watch **Teaching Video Two**.

☐ Listen to the question and answer video.

☐ Listen to the optional energy healing audio recordings:
   ☐ Chakra Clearing and Healing
   ☐ Finding High Vibration
   ☐ Rooting and Grounding Meditation

HOLDING THE STATE OF *Oneness*

Once you are able to feel the state of Oneness, you feel a tingly energy above your head. You feel a string attached to your head like it's lifting you towards the sky. Your body feels like it's becoming one with the air surrounding you, as you begin to feel your expansiveness. You go deeper and begin to feel that the body itself does not restrict your energy; you can feel out of the body; you can feel Oneness with everything, everywhere.

Once you can feel this energy, the next step is to learn to hold that state as you're living your life. Many find it easy to hold the vibration of Oneness while they are doing mindless activities (which require no thought) like chores around the house, cooking, walking, getting ready in the morning, physically shopping in a store, brushing your teeth, etc.

Your homework in week two is to practice holding Oneness as you go about mindless activities throughout your day. Remember, you are never to meditate or practice Oneness while driving, operating machinery or the like. This week:

1. Continue getting into Oneness for one minute morning, noon, and night by saying the Oneness Meditation words to yourself within.

2. When you are doing chores around the house, getting ready in the morning and at night, brushing your teeth, and moving your body (walking, stretching, etc)—bring your attention back to Oneness. Ask, "Oneness, are you still there?" Feel that your heart is one with your body, that both are one with the air surrounding you. Feel Oneness with all life on Earth and All That Is, everywhere.

3. If it becomes difficult to return to Oneness, try breathing deeply. Be conscious of your breath in and out, in and out, as instructed on page 24.

4. While in Oneness, hold this state by continuing to keep your attention on that feeling of expansiveness as you breathe and do mindless activities.

Set yourself up for success by looking at your schedule and routines throughout your weekdays and weekends. Do you have blocks of time throughout your week when you are focused on mindless activity?

Use the space below to write down where you have blocks of time in your schedule and make it more of a routine to practice holding Oneness during these times. Expanding the length of time you're in Oneness throughout your day will help you build muscle memory (or better yet, *brain memory*) and hold this vibration more steadily throughout your life.

Look at your schedule. When do you have blocks of time to practice holding Oneness? It may be mornings when you're getting ready for your day, weekends, or at night when you're cleaning up. What days and times work best for you?

_____

_____

_____

_____

_____

_____

_____

_____

_____

_____

_____

_____

_____

_____

WHAT HAPPENS WHEN
I COME OUT OF ONENESS?

Many students ask, "Julie, what happens when my mind wanders or my energy shifts, and I come out of a state of Oneness?" Here's what I tell them: do you know what it's like to be cold in your home when you're relaxing? I've had this happen several times when I'm in my house, and to warm myself up I put a blanket around my body all the way up to my shoulders. At some point that blanket will start to slip down off my shoulders, and I inevitably take the blanket and pull it back up so I'm completely covered in warmth.

Holding Oneness is like continuing to pull a warm blanket up to cover you. It's not frustrating or aggravating. You simply notice when you're cold and when you are, your mind recognizes the blanket has fallen, so you pull it up. Easy and effortless, right? It's the same with Oneness.

You start your day with the Oneness Meditation each morning and then you go about your day. You take a shower, make the kids breakfast, go to dry your hair and as you're engaged in these mindless activities, check in on Oneness from time to time. Say, "Hello Oneness? Are you still there?" And immediately you get a sense of warm tingles surrounding your body and Oneness radiating from your heart expanding out to the world and beyond.

Oneness, in fact, IS still there even when your consciousness is not concentrating on feeling it. When you practice this long enough, you end up checking in several times an hour and you feel Oneness more and more as you are "doing" in your life. I want you to get to the point where Oneness becomes your natural state of being. Ask yourself a few times an hour, "Oneness, are you still there?" And immediately tap into that vibration which surrounds you, is you, expands from you allowing you to be one with All That Is.

BENEFITS OF ONENESS

Practicing Oneness is like living your life in a meditative state. We know the benefits of meditation are plentiful. According to healthline.com, meditation helps:

- Reduce cortisol (the stress hormone)
- Reduce anxiety
- Improve self-image and a more positive outlook on life
- Develop a stronger understanding of yourself, helping you grow into your best self
- Lengthen your attention span
- Reduce age-related memory loss
- Increase positive emotion and actions toward yourself and others
- Improve sleep
- Reduce blood pressure
- And more

Have you noticed any benefits of meditation in your life after practicing Oneness the past two weeks? What have you noticed? If you have not noticed any benefits yet, reflect on that below and write what benefits you hope Oneness will bring into your life. Continue practicing Oneness and live in expectation that you will see those benefits soon.

_____

_____

_____

_____

_____

_____

_____

_____

_____

_____

ONENESS AND THE OTHER SIDE

When you feel Oneness, the crown chakra above your head is open and this means you are in your soul's frequency and in alignment with God, your loved ones on the Other Side, your Angels, and your Higher Self. When you are in Oneness, the voice of your Egoic Mind quiets and the voice of your intuition becomes clearer. You become a clear channel like a radio station without any static background noise.

I want you to understand this now, because as you hold Oneness you may begin to notice you're already hearing your intuition more clearly. That's amazing and I'm so happy for you! You're learning to connect with God, pray and ask questions, and know what it's like to get a more clear response! Now anywhere you go in life, the answers you need are always within you and that brings a deep sense of peace.

If you're not, don't worry! Students come to me at every phase of their spiritual awakening. Some have been practicing for years, and some are new to spiritual concepts. Believe me when I tell you that the only way to fail is to stop trying. If you keep persisting, your angels will help you get where you are going.

FEELING OTHERS' ENERGY

At times, another by-product of Oneness is feeling other people's energy. Here's what you need to know: it is unethical to try to tap into the energy of someone who has not given you permission. It's not okay to poke around in other people's business. While we do not do this, there may be instances where you did not intend to feel someone's energy, but it was with you regardless.

Once at a "Game of Thrones" party with friends one night, the men were in the kitchen and the women were in the living room. I was at my best friend's house, but I did not know most of the other people there. I was in mid-conversation with the ladies when I looked at a woman I'd just met and out of my mouth flew the words, "Who is the fatherly figure on the Other Side? He needs you to know he's with you." She broke down crying and said, "My grandfather. He just passed away this week!" I was able to bring through messages for her that evening and it brought her some peace.

Friend, I want you to know that this can happen, but a special word of warning: this book does not train you, neither does the Angel Membership program allow or give you permission to bring through information to other people from Spirit. This book and the Angel Membership are strictly to help you learn to work with Spirit in order to aid you in connecting with information for your own personal life.

Only my Angel Reiki School trains individuals to use their God-given spiritual gifts. If you are considering doing this work as a career, you need training because you will occasionally come across people who are suicidal. People may ask you to tell them if they should leave their marriage, move across the country, or adopt a baby. Spirit will not bypass a person's freewill by telling them what to do, and neither should any trained intuitive energy healer. I make a practice of not telling clients what choice to make. A good training program like my Angel Reiki School is going to teach you what to do in those situations and when to refer to a therapist or other medical professional, which I often do!

Bringing through messages is not some whimsical thing you do for "fun." It is very serious. You cannot and should not take this work lightly. Please respect the difference. If you want to learn to develop your spiritual gifts and do this work as a career, you must go through training. That training does not need to be with me, but be sure you're clear on what you'll be receiving and learning before you sign up for a program.

Most energy healing programs do not teach you to develop your unique spiritual gifts, and most mediumship/intuitive programs do not teach energy work; however, the two flow together hand-in-hand. That's why Archangel Haniel channeled the Angel Reiki School through me, to teach people how to open up to all of their spiritual gifts and use them to serve others. My students say, "Julie, I've taken all the Reiki levels before, and been to different spiritual and self-help retreats—none of it clicked until I took the Angel Reiki School." That is the best compliment I could receive! If you'd like to learn more about developing your spiritual gifts in my training program, I invite you to check out the Angel Reiki School details at: www.theangelmedium.com

SENDING OTHERS ONENESS

There is a difference between trying to tap into another person's energy and wanting to send someone positive energy to help them. When I was young we had a station wagon and my sister and I often sat in the very back, looking out of the rear of the car. I remember wanting to stop for every broken down car we passed. When I learned from my parents that it was not possible to stop and help everyone, I heard a voice within me say, "Send them love." I brought my hands together in prayer position near my heart then pointed my hands to the people we passed who needed support. I imagined enormous love flowing through my heart, through my hands, and out to each person. I was doing energy healing and talking to Spirit as a kid and didn't realize it. You can send anyone God's energy with the intent of helping that person and doing God's Will.

It's one thing to bring through messages without training (which we don't do), but when your intention is to help another by simply sending them love, Oneness, God-energy, angels, and supportive energy—that is different, because it is energy in flow (the same as prayer) and that is allowed. When we come together, pray for one another, and send loving energy to one another, it can work miracles.

Here is an example: Laurie needs support because she's going through a rough time in her life. Due to all she's going through, her energy is depleted. Five people use their freewill to send Laurie God's energy and pray for God to send angels to her side. These five people are not sending Laurie their own energy (because it is a limited resource), they're sending her God's energy (which is unlimited). Laurie now has a mass of God's energy and angels surrounding her in every direction. This energy is now able to assist her significantly because the five people used their freewill to help. It is important to be Earth angels to one another by (first and foremost) taking action in life when possible, then sending God's love, asking for God's support, and by asking for God to send angels. This is work you should do whenever you can!

ONENESS, CHERUBS AND OTHER ANGELS

In this book, after practicing Oneness for four weeks I'm going to teach you how to communicate with your angels for the purpose of hearing your messages (regarding your own life) more clearly. This is where things can get complex. Oneness is the tool you need to communicate with your angels, just as you use a radio to hear a station. However, the angels themselves will help you learn how to feel and hold Oneness too! Angels are God's energy extending out to help us souls the way rays of energy come off the sun.

When you ask God for help getting into Oneness, angels are assigned to help you! In fact, it is the Cherubim Angels' (aka, cherubs') job to hold the energy of Oneness open for you to get into at any time.

Here's how this works. You have 37.2+ trillion cells in your body and Spirit says you have 37.2+ trillion atoms surrounding you within your auric field (74.4+ trillion total). Imagine all of these cells and atoms as dots within you and surrounding you. When you look in the mirror with your human eyes, you see the outline of your own body and lines that define where the body ends. However, if you took a step back and looked at your body and auric field like a bunch of pixelated dots, you wouldn't be able to see where your body ends and where your auric field begins because all of the energy would be flowing together.

In order to understand the Cherubim, you must look at this picture from a three-dimensional perspective. Imagine that you look at your body from a side angle and all of these dots now become straws from a three-dimensional perspective. Now, when you see the 74.4+ trillion dots within you and surrounding you, from the side angle they actually look like 74.4+ trillion straws put together. Spirit says these combined straws are more representative of what the energy of Oneness looks like. One side of the straw opens to the energy of the Earth realm. The straw's tube is actually "the tunnel" people talk about in near death experiences. And the other side of the straw opens to the Other Side, Heaven and God's energy. When the straws are open at both ends, you have an open connection. You are able to tap into and hold Oneness with every cell in your body and every atom surrounding you.

You are in alignment. Pause and feel that for a moment, you are able to feel Oneness with every cell of your being and every atom surrounding you. As you imagine this, I want you to feel an instantaneous access to Oneness and feel that you are one with All That Is.

So what stops you from feeling Oneness? The Egoic Mind. The Egoic Mind acts as a cap over the end of each straw. Spirit says it is like a lid on top of a pot, except you have 74.4+ trillion pots and your Egoic Mind can cap all of them simultaneously with one large lid at any time. Fear, division, duality, anxiety, stress, and every emotion produced by the Egoic Mind acts as a lid restricting the flow of Oneness between you and the Other Side.

Have you ever put a pot of water with a lid on a stove to boil? If you don't catch it in time, the water will bubble up and the lid will begin to bounce up and down a bit, creating a crack where the hot steam can escape. The analogy illustrates what it's like for your angels and loved ones to be a part of your Spirit Team. Your Egoic Mind and freewill are the lid you can place instantly on all 74.4+ trillion straws connecting you to God. Your Spirit Team, God, your angels, your loved ones, and guides never give up on you when you close the lid. They love you unconditionally and fight for you to remain connected now and always. Your Spirit Team is always doing what they can to keep Oneness energy pushing against the lid of the Egoic Mind so that even through the tiniest crack, you can feel Oneness and always remember your path back to God.

Friend, here's what you need to realize: your freewill choice acts as the decider of those cap lids. When you say, "No," or "I can't," or "It works for other people, but it's not going to work for me," you have decided to put that lid back on all 74.4+ trillion straws and remain disconnected. It is your choice. Spirit keeps pushing and rooting for you, but those beliefs limit them in a major way. When you say, "God, I don't know how you're going to do this, but I need a miracle. Please help me with _____," God is able to come through with every resource. They have because you've just used your freewill to lift every lid and choose to connect to Source.

As you learn to feel and hold Oneness, ask God to work miracles in your life. Invite God, the Cherubim, all your angels, loved ones, and guides on the Other Side to use every resource available to them to help you hold Oneness throughout your day, every day of your life. When you ask for help and believe that help is on its way, you'll see your life shift in positive ways you didn't know were possible.

IS REIKI ENERGY DIFFERENT FROM ONENESS?

What is described as Reiki energy is simply God's energy or Oneness. It is all the same energy, though teachers around the world have many names for it. While the words may be different, the energy itself is the same. It is All That Is. It's God. As a teacher, I used to use the words "high vibration" to describe Oneness, but I found it often caused people to feel the energy above their head but stopped them from feeling the energy everywhere (within their body radiating out to everything everywhere). They did not feel Oneness with All That Is because they only felt it above their heads. When I say Oneness, there is a fuller, all-encompassing energy that students feel. That is what I want you to feel, so that is the word I now use.

WHAT ABOUT NEGATIVE ENERGIES?

Yesterday, I was giving a reading to a young woman in a session. She came into our meeting so upset and said, "I know that I am supposed to be a healer too, but I went to a different medium last month and she told me that energy healing and feeling Oneness will open me up to negative energies. She told me not to do it. I'm so confused."

First, learning how to get into and hold Oneness is learning to connect with God and feel God's energy alone. There are low vibrations here on Earth, but they are only in this physical realm. There is no low vibration in Heaven.

None of the work I do is low vibrational in any way. Nor is any of the work I teach you to do. We only connect to God's energy. If you are concerned about tapping into low vibrations here on Earth, all you have to do to shield and protect yourself is pray this prayer:

"God, please only let me connect to your energy and any beings that walk in your energy. God, I ask you to ensure that as I work to connect with you more deeply, I only connect with your energy now and for the rest of my life. Please transmute any low vibrational frequencies I encounter in my life into love energy."

Trust, have faith, believe that it is so, and it is.

Sadly, I've personally witnessed both celebrity mediums and local healers discourage capable students from becoming healers. When I see this happen, I pray and ask God to send these healers an abundance of Oneness energy. I also ask God to build the strength and confidence in all souls on Earth who are to become healers. I ask God to ensure nothing stands in the way of their souls' purpose.

When a healer stops another healer from becoming who they're meant to be, it holds our entire planet back from making huge shifts. If another healer ever tells you something that doesn't resonate with you, do not take, believe, or accept that energy.

It is important for you to protect your energy. When it comes to your spiritual awakening, anything that does not resonate with you is not your truth. Work with healers who only connect with God's energy and bring through positive, loving messages. Before you book an appointment with an intuitive, psychic medium, angel reader, etc. you have the right to ask them, "Do you bring through negative information? Do you believe in connecting with God's energy alone? Or do you open yourself up to the low vibration of Earth and anything that comes through?" Ask any other questions that arise within you and then make your decision on whether or not this is a person you want to work with.

Many times in meditation, Spirit has shown me that our spiritual health will soon become just as much a priority as our mental, emotional, and physical health. Spirit says that the number of people who attend church will most likely continue to drastically decrease over the next 25 years (as it has since the 1980's) because religion has not made necessary changes to keep its patrons and their children safe from sexual predators, patriarchy, racism, extremism, and much more that is still deeply rooted in many religious institutions. I pray to see these religious institutions take an unwavering stance on sexual predators; create intentional reformation to be inclusive of all people as they truly are; and ensure complete equality among their leadership. Some institutions have taken these steps, and I pray that all move in this direction.

I'm telling you this because the angel, Saraphina (about whom we will talk more in the later chapters on Angel Communication), says there will be 14 waves of spiritual healers in our lifetime and that as of 2021, we are on the third wave. That is to say, there is much work to be done and many more healers are needed. Just as there are many churches in your area and counselors in your town, the need for local spiritual teachers who are God-based is rising—and it is in part the work of all us healers combined, serving and teaching others, that will help shift the planet.

Your work is deeply needed and you are deeply needed. If you are called to be an energy healer, intuitive, or develop your spiritual gifts, you have to know that there is room for all. Don't let anyone tell you otherwise—you must follow your heart!

ONENESS
Week Three

Continue practicing the Oneness Meditation

for three minutes every day: One minute when you wake up, one minute at lunch, and one minute before bed. Practice holding Oneness during conversations.

If you're in the Angel Membership,

go to the Oneness course:

☐ Watch the **Teaching Video Three.**

☐ Listen to optional energy healing audio recordings:
    ☐ Bedtime Meditation
    ☐ Morning Meditation
    ☐ Practicing Oneness Part I

ONENESS DURING CONVERSATIONS

The first week of this program, you practiced getting into and feeling Oneness. Last week, you practiced holding the vibration of Oneness while engaged in mindless activities. This week, you're going to hold Oneness during conversations with friends, family, your roommate/s, strangers you meet and colleagues.

Think about all the conversations you have each day and each week. It's not only easy to be in a conversation and hold Oneness, but it is super fun and it lovingly raises the vibrations of others without them realizing it. It happens automatically without you even trying.

When you are in a state of Oneness, you are holding the highest vibrational frequency that is and you become a tuning fork. Have you ever seen a metal tuning fork? You hit the tuning fork and it vibrates at a specific frequency. This is what musicians use to tune their instruments. Humans are the same. By simply holding Oneness around others, you can literally tune the energy of another human being without trying.

How does this happen? Think back to page 36 when you learned how the Cherubs' energy works like 74.4 trillion straws keeping you open and connected to God's energy, but the Egoic Mind wants to put a lid at the end of each of those straws in order to keep you in vibrations of fear, stress, and anxiety. Let's estimate that over 90% of people in the world live 99% of their everyday life in that dense Egoic Mind state where all 74.4 trillion straws are capped with lids so that they cannot feel God's energy with ease. Most humans are not conscious they are doing this, nor are they aware they have a choice to live a different way. All they know is that they constantly feel bad. When you hold Oneness, and go to lunch with a friend who spends most of their day in the dense energy of the Egoic Mind, all of a sudden they are surrounded by your energy (which feels like God's openness, love, joy, ease, and grace) and their vibration rises.

When you hold Oneness, you are emitting the highest vibration that is, which means anyone near you is a receiver of that vibration. If their vibration is low, immersing yourself in Oneness will tune them up to a higher frequency by helping them to awaken at their own pace, over time. This isn't something you need to make an effort to achieve, you need only reside in Oneness and the tuning/awakening will happen on its own. It does not matter if you're right next to the person, over Zoom, communicating via social media. Everything you do emits a vibrational frequency and when you hold Oneness as you speak, you help others to tune to this vibration.

DO NOT ENGAGE IN LOW VIBRATIONAL CONVERSATIONS

You need to be aware of the topics you talk about with others to better observe how it shifts your energy (and theirs). Have you ever gone to lunch with a friend and gossiped about people or happenings? I've done this in the past, and each time—wham!—I was immediately sucked back down into a very low vibration. Does that mean that we need to throw away our friends for new ones? Absolutely not! Though it may mean that we need to have conversations with these friends to suggest we steer clear of gossip and topics that lower the energy.

A girlfriend and I had this conversation years ago, after which, we both looked at each other and said, "Ugh, I feel horrible, and sticky now. Ick! Our conversations don't normally leave me feeling this way." We agreed that we had evolved as human beings and our conversations would have to evolve as well. Now we are accountability partners in our conversations, helping one another to keep things positive where we can. We allow one another to talk honestly and openly about our own feelings and life challenges, but we no longer gossip. It's our own personal rule and we both leave our conversations feeling uplifted in Oneness.

Now, I'm not telling you to keep everything positive to the point of bypassing conversations or life topics that are difficult. It's the opposite. You must be direct. There are hugely damaging and harmful injustices in this world, that no amount of love and high vibration can change, alone. Action is necessary. Discernment is also necessary. Give yourself grace and ask God for help to know when it is best to simply send love, do something, or say something. Trust that God will show you the way.

PRACTICE ONENESS WHILE IN CONVERSATION

Have you ever been in a conversation with another person and they say something that is similar to an experience you had, so you begin thinking about what you're going to say next when they stop speaking? When you're in Oneness, you're connected to God's infinite divine knowledge and you no longer have to do this. When you're holding Oneness in a conversation and it is your turn to speak, you really do not have to think about what to say. God places a loving intuitive thought within you when it is time to speak, and the conversation continues to flow!

HOLDING ONENESS IN CONVERSATION

I want you use conscious awareness, to practice holding the state of Oneness while speaking to others for one week as follows:

1. Continue to get into Oneness for one minute morning, noon, and night by saying the Oneness Meditation words to yourself within.

2. Continue to hold Oneness while engaging in mindless activity.

3. Be aware of Oneness while you are in conversation or speaking with others. Simply breathe deeply while you are in conversation and be aware of the energy of Oneness and the conversation itself. Again, you no longer need to plan what you will say ahead of time in your mind. When it is your turn to speak, what you are to say will just be there. For a refresher on how to breathe deeply, please go back to page 24.

ONENESS DOESN'T MAKE YOUR LIFE MAGICALLY PERFECT

You Still Have To Do Your Work

Once I learned to feel and hold Oneness, I expected my life to be magically perfect. I expected not to feel low vibrations or emotions in general anymore. I was under the assumption that spiritual teachers were perfect, and if I was not, I was doing something wrong. I thought this way because, socially, teachers are placed on a pedestal. We believe that if you are a celebrity, royalty, head of a company, author or teacher, that you are in that position because you have achieved a level of perfection others have not, but this is not true.

Being human means being imperfect and continually responding to life's challenges. If you want to teach one day, you must accept that you will always be both teacher and student. It is the call of every human being to be both teacher and student their entire lives.

Do not expect Oneness to make your life perfect. Do not expect to live in Oneness 24/7, 365. Even world-renowned spiritual teacher, Eckhart Tolle, has said there are moments (however briefly) where he comes out of this state (he calls "The Now"). We can't reach a level of perfection on Earth because everyone has an Egoic Mind in this realm: it is part of life on Earth. You can find ways to work with your Egoic Mind and limit its dominance over you, but having mixed emotions, having life challenges, and having ups and downs is normal.

You are not bad, wrong, or less than for ebbing and flowing in and out of Oneness—this simply makes you human. When you become aware that you are not in Oneness, you can redirect your attention back to feeling God's loving energy surrounding you and flowing through you.

FEELINGS AND ONENESS

You'll find that as you go through life, you'll have a range of different emotional experiences. If you were to lose someone close to you, you would experience the emotions of grief, loss, and intense sadness. There can also be past pain and emotional traumas that are triggered, causing us to feel anger, frustration, and fear.

These feelings indicate that you need to spend some time sitting with the emotions within you, allowing them to be with you and move through you. The angels say the quickest way to release your feelings is to spend time with them, allowing those feelings to genuinely be with you.

When I'm feeling low vibrational emotions, I practice the following process to return to Oneness. Archangel Gabrielle taught me this process and we'll talk about that more in the chapters on Angel Communication. For now, try this process for yourself:

1. Sit with your feelings and emotions in meditation. Allow them to be with you. Do not judge them. Do not believe the feelings. Just acknowledge them.

2. Specifically define the emotion you're feeling. Ask yourself: What am I feeling? Allow the answer to come to you. Then ask yourself: Where do I feel this inside my body? If you are not used to feeling your own energy, you may have to google "list of feelings" or "list of emotions" so you can clearly name what you are feeling within, beyond the vagueness of "sadness," "anxiety," "fear," etc. Are you feeling: overwhelmed, panicky, shamed, betrayed, belittled, lonely, criticized, powerless? The more you look at these lists and ask, "What

am I feeling?" the easier and faster this process will become, and the better you will know yourself and your own energy!

3. Once you know the specific emotion, you can go within your mind to find the thought that is causing the feeling. Ask yourself: "What thought within my mind or what experience did I have that is causing me to feel this?" Friend, any feeling can always be tied to a thought or experience you've had. For example, I may be married with a child and still feel lonely. I feel this loneliness because I've been devoting too much time to work, and not enough to my family.

4. When you know what thought or experience is causing you to feel your emotion, you can answer the deeper question, "What do I need?" When I do this, I bring God in and ask, "God, what would you have me do?" The answer I hear back is different each time. Sometimes I need to say something, other times I need to do something, and sometimes I just need to let things go. Expect to get a different answer every time you ask this question.

5. Next, take action. Use your throat chakra to speak aloud what you need. Whether you are letting go, saying something, or doing something, these are all actionable steps. When you take action for yourself or speak your needs, you are allowing pent-up energy in the throat chakra and body to be released. This calms your nervous system and allows your physical body to come back into Oneness.

6. I believe in and encourage you to work with a counselor or therapist regularly because, as humans, we have ups and downs hundreds of times throughout our days. As my friend, Grace Boland, once said on the podcast, "Working with a counselor or therapist helps us to sort, fold, and put away our mental laundry." She's right—you can feel it energetically! Counselors and therapists help us feel as if all our mental laundry is organized, leaving us with more mental capacity for everything that calls to us within our hearts!

WHAT HAPPENS WHEN I'M NOT IN ONENESS?

When you are not in Oneness, it simply means your attention (your conscious awareness) is not on the energy of your soul. I've asked Spirit about this many times, and They explain it like this: If you are a parent who is not physically near your child (ie, the child is at school or some other place), does that mean the child is no longer yours? No! Of course not. In the same way, when your attention is not on Oneness, that does not mean Oneness has left you or that Oneness is gone or not yours anymore. You can get back into that state at any time. It's simply that in that particular moment, your conscious awareness is on something else and that happens in life.

You have two choices, beat yourself up for it or let it go and simply return to Oneness. Anytime you beat yourself up, it is not from your soul self. It is from your Egoic Mind space. So don't do that! Allow yourself to be in flow and go, "Oh! I'm not in Oneness right now. Okay God and Cherubs, can you help me return to Oneness?" They will help you to feel Oneness instantaneously and it's as easy as that! No need to beat yourself up. Simply stay in a state of loving yourself and being kind to yourself.

CAN ONENESS BE TAKEN AWAY FROM ME?

Many students question, "Can Oneness be taken away from me? Or can someone else steal it from me?" They worry that a person might send negative energy to them, restricting them from feeling Oneness in the future, but this is impossible.

Oneness is the energy of your soul. It is your birthright and can never be taken away from you, because it is you. There is no one and no thing in this world that could direct negative energy your way to stop you from feeling Oneness. It is yours always.

There can be times when life is overwhelming: planning a wedding; moving; completing an important work project; grieving the loss of someone you loved; dealing with health issues. There are times in life where we can go through big life challenges. During these times, our awareness may be distracted and the intensity of the situation makes our energy feel heavy. These are great times to get an Angel Reiki Energy Healing session. I've included the following Angel Reiki Energy Healing videos in the Angel Membership, Oneness eCourse, for you to use at any time to clear your energy and make feeling Oneness easier:

The Oneness Meditation

Chakra Clearing and Healing

Bedtime Meditation

Morning Meditation

"Be One" Meditation

Turning Past Pain Into Love

Practicing Oneness Part 1

Practicing Oneness Part 2

WHY SPIRITUAL PRACTICE IS NECESSARY

When life gets distracting, our thoughts, feelings, and emotions pull us in more directions than ever before. Take advertisements alone, for example: in the 70's, a single person could encounter up to 1,600 ads per day. In 2007, the average person saw 5,000 ads per day. Today, the average person now encounters between 6,000 and 10,000 ads—every day.

Each ad has the ability within less than a second to cause you to have a thought, feeling, or even take a different course of action that day. Now add text messages, emails, your job, news, music apps, online shopping, home voice devices, not to mention actual people in your life, or the fact that these algorithms' sole job is to reward you for leaving your physical interactions with others to go back into the online world.

Friend, never in your lifetime have you been more bombarded with outside forces than you are today, but no one is going to come take that phone out of your hand. The plain truth is that Oneness requires your attention. If you do not prioritize your attention to Oneness, it will absolutely fade off into the background and you will feel it less. Instead of feeling the love, bliss, and grace of Oneness you've come to experience as part of your every day, you will revert back to feel all the stressors, anxieties, and fears again.

A spiritual practice is a ritual or routine that aids your spiritual health. Spiritual practice is prioritizing Oneness with the same consistency that you shower and brush your teeth. Those are practices you do routinely to aid the health of your body. A spiritual practice is a ritual or routine that aids your spiritual health.

The instructor of a meditation course I took once reported that a good night's rest reduces your cortisol levels by 8–10%, whereas a consistent meditative practice can reduce your cortisol levels by 30–40%. If true, that is huge!

I want you to see this visually, the way that Spirit shows me. See your body, and in front of you is a pile of trash swirling around your body in your auric field. That is the energy of distraction we live in every day. Now, if you take away 30–40% of that trash swirl, you're going to feel more spacious, airy, and so much better—that is what spiritual practice does for you.

Everyone's spiritual practice looks different. You can choose to start every day with twenty minutes in Oneness. You can choose to do three minutes a day (morning, noon, and night) by saying the words to yourself. You can learn to hold Oneness while engaged in mindless activity and while holding conversations. You might even integrate all three. Regardless, the more you hold Oneness and the less trash you feel swirling around you, the better you feel. The better you feel, the more you will see those positive results in your life.

What will your spiritual practice be? Be realistic with yourself. What do you have time for? How can you prioritize Oneness in your life? Take a few moments to breathe deeply, then write down what ideas flow to you:

_____

_____

_____

_____

_____

_____

_____

_____

I want you to expect your life to be full of abundance in career, family, friends, love, health, and every area of your life. At the same time, I want you to have a plan for days when you need to recenter because you are distracted by the swirl of life. On those days, you may think to yourself, "I need more time in Oneness." Create a plan to identify when you are distracted and how you will recenter by getting back into Oneness.

_____

_____

_____

_____

_____

_____

_____

_____

ESSENTIAL OILS AND VIBRATIONAL MUSIC ENHANCE ONENESS

Both essential oils and vibrational music enhance your ability to hold Oneness. When you dab one of your favorite essential oils on your wrists or neck, you will catch a hint of that smell periodically throughout the day. As you smell your favorite scent, your awareness will automatically shift back to Oneness. You take a deep breath and you're in oneness again! Wearing essential oils is one way to train your brain and begin to stay in the vibration consistently.

Always select your favorite scent. I often wear sandalwood on my wrists and neck as perfume. I also make spray bottles of my favorite scent (a mixture of patchouli, sandalwood, and clove), and spray them around the house or as perfume. I buy spray bottles and essential oils at my local health food store. I fill the bottle 3/4th of the way full with rubbing alcohol and then add 20 drops of sandalwood, 15 drops of clove and 5 drops of patchouli. While I like my sprays strong (sometimes adding more), many people love a light scent with just 5 drops of each. You can play with the mixture and find what you love most. Some people swap the rubbing alcohol for a low-quality vodka as a base instead.

Vibrational music has a similar effect as essential oils in opening your energy to Oneness.

You can go to YouTube and search "love hz" or "high vibrational music" to find many songs that hold a high vibration. When you listen to them, it's like a key that opens your 74.4 trillion straw-like portals to Oneness and keeps you in the vibration throughout your day. Test out different essential oils and vibrational songs, and have fun with it! Use what works for you and discard what doesn't.

WHAT HAPPENS WHEN LIFE GETS OVERWHELMING?

The Power of "I am" Statements

In the Bible, when man asks God, "What is your name?" God replies, "I am." These two little words carry the expansive, airy feeling of Oneness. Say it over and over to yourself slowly. *I am. I am. I am.*

When you practice Oneness regularly, expect to become more aware of your thoughts throughout your day. As life gets overwhelming, "I am" statements can help. You are saying to yourself, "In this moment right now, I am safe. I am secure." This will bring you an unparalleled feeling of safety and security.

Positive "I am" statements (and affirmation statements in general), can help you override negative thoughts within you. For example:

Initial Thought	I Am Statement
I am not good enough.	I am enough!
I am not the size I want to be.	I am the most fit I've ever been!
I am not loved.	I am loved.
I don't know who I am.	I know and love who I am.
I am stuck.	I communicate my feelings and needs in every conversation.
My partner doesn't love me.	My partner and I share emotional intimacy daily through talk and touch.
Bad things happen to me.	I always attract only the best circumstances and positive people in my life.
I hate exercise.	I enjoy moving my body, stretching and strengthening my muscles.
It's chaotic around here.	I surround myself with peaceful people.
I hate my coworker.	My work environment is calm and peaceful.
I am so stressed out.	Every day, I am more and more at ease.
I don't like meditation.	Being calm and relaxed energizes my whole being.

What are three negative thoughts you think regularly?

1.

2.

3.

Let's see how you can rework them into three new positive "I Am" statements or affirmations:

1.

2.

3.

If you need help, join my Angel Membership and go to the community where you can write a post and get feedback from peers.

CAN I TEACH OTHERS ONENESS?

In order for the vibration of our planet to rise, we must all learn how to hold Oneness. Once we have it down, we must teach it to others. Please tell others about all you've learned from this book, course, and podcast! You have my permission to share the Oneness Meditation alone with others in your life or your classes (with proper attribution, and excluding my other copyrighted work, writings, videos, etc)!

The more people who learn to hold Oneness, the better.

If you teach Oneness, never allow your students to believe that you yourself are the way to Oneness. You are not the way, you are a tool that helps them to remember their true energy. It is every person's divine right to feel Oneness. Their Oneness is not attached to you as the teacher. Oneness is the essence of the souls you teach; it is who and what they truly are.

Some of my students say, "Julie, I only feel Oneness when I'm working with you." I'll tell them, "Please don't think that way. You don't need me. You *are* Oneness, and you can get into this energy at any time by yourself."

People will say this to you too. Remember, it is their Egoic Mind telling them they need someone outside of themselves to feel Oneness, but this is simply untrue. If someone says this to you, you must show them that the energy they are feeling is their soul's energy and they do not need any other person to feel this. You can help guide others to experience Oneness, but they do not require your continued presence to feel and hold Oneness each day. That is their birthright!

ONENESS
Week Four

Continue practicing the Oneness Meditation

for three minutes every day: One minute when you wake up, one minute at lunch, and one minute before bed. Practice holding Oneness while "doing," to better understand that there isn't any moment where you are separate from All That Is. At every moment of doing, thinking, talking, speaking, being—*you are one with All That Is*.

If you're in the Angel Membership,
go to the Oneness course:

☐ Watch **Teaching Video Four.**

☐ Watch the question and answer video.

☐ Listen to optional energy healing audio recordings:
    ☐ "Be One With All That Is" Meditation
    ☐ Turning Past Pain Into Love
    ☐ Practicing Oneness Part II

HOLDING ONENESS WHILE DOING

Friend, you've done such a great job! It's time to put together all that you've learned. For one week, I want you to practice holding Oneness while sending emails, while working on projects, while doing everything in your life (remember: do not practice any form of meditation, including the Oneness Meditation, while you are driving, working with machinery or in situations requiring mental alertness).

It's time for you to open yourself to the fact that you can never be separate from All That Is. Every moment of doing, thinking, talking, speaking, being—you are one.

When I first tried this, my Egoic Mind came in saying, "You cannot 'do' and hold Oneness at the same time. It's not possible!" I felt it was hard to hold Oneness while checking my work email and focusing on projects. But the truth is that it is absolutely possible to hold Oneness and 'do.' We may need to slow down our energy and be more aware of our thoughts, but it is possible to 'do' and 'be' at the same time.

Your mind may want to make this difficult by telling you, "It's not possible." I want you to remember the Cherubs and how they are working with you. Remember that the only energy which disconnects you from God and Oneness is the Egoic Mind—that's it. When you are aware of Oneness, your thoughts, and energy throughout the day, you are proactively lifting the lid of the Egoic Mind off of the 74.4 trillion cells and atoms that surround you and are you. Doing this allows the Cherubs to direct Oneness, divine wisdom, God-energy, love, joy, peace, bliss, ease, and grace through those 74.4 trillion straws: it's palpable.

God's energy is palpable and you can indeed feel Oneness as you go about your daily life.

Remind yourself—Oneness cannot include any binary of any kind, by the very nature of its essence. Oneness, meaning everything interconnected, and leaving nothing out. The Egoic Mind is the opposite of Oneness, (which you must remember when it starts telling you what isn't possible in Oneness).

AFTER THE ECSTASY, DO THE LAUNDRY

There are different stages of spiritual awakening. For those who've never felt Oneness before this book, this is brand new. Some may have experienced Oneness before, but learned how to hold it from this book. Here's what you need to know: when some people get into the energy of Oneness, they wish they could take a vacation for half a year and just be in this energy. There are even some spiritual teachers who will encourage their students to run away into the mountains, leave their families, and hold this energy 24/7, 365.

Here's why you cannot run off and seclude yourself in the mountains: Imagine that tomorrow, one million parents spiritually awakened to Oneness and a spiritual teacher told them, "The only way to hold this energy is to leave your friends and family behind, so that you have zero distractions and you can learn to hold this energy all the time, your whole life." Friend, you may think I'm being funny, but I was told to do this at the beginning of my training, and I know others who listened to teachers like this and left their families to do so. What I want you to understand is that this is not okay. What would happen to the children they left behind? Millions of children would grow up hating spirituality, hating awakening, hating Oneness because it destroyed their family.

Holding the energy of Oneness and helping this planet raise the vibration does not mean abandoning your life. It means we must integrate and infuse our new wisdom of Oneness, joy, love, bliss, and ease into our current world. Just by holding this energy yourself, others around you will notice that you changed, you are different in an amazing way. They will come to you and ask you why you're glowing, and if you'll teach them how to hold Oneness, so they can glow like you do. Over the years, your friends' vibrations will rise, your kids' and partners' vibrations will rise and your world will shift in a way that will allow you to see the positive benefit that Oneness has on everyone around you.

Similarly, the Egoic Mind can act out when you begin to hold Oneness more and more. It may tell you, "But I don't want to do anything except stay in this yummy energy. I don't want to do the laundry, I don't want to fold the clothes." When this happens, friend, it means that you are at a point where you are now learning how to integrate Oneness into your life and this is wonderful. Remember, Oneness and doing are not separate things, they're one. Any time your mind tries to come in and tell you that you cannot hold Oneness while doing, it is trying to bring division and separation energy back to you. You must talk back to that voice within your mind and tell it, "No, dear teenager in my head, you don't understand. I can do the laundry and fold the clothes and work on a project for my job all while remaining in Oneness. I can do anything and remain in Oneness."

Spiritual teacher, Jack Kornfield has an amazing book called, *After the Ecstasy, the Laundry*. The entire book is about incorporating Oneness back into your life. If you need help with this, I highly recommend this book as it focuses exclusively on this topic.

ONENESS WILL SHIFT YOUR LIFE

Oneness led me to change every aspect of my life: my marriage, career, friendships, relationship with my daughter, hobbies, home. When you begin to hold Oneness more and more in your life, you begin to vibrate at the highest vibration and some things from your life before no longer resonate with you.

There are two roads to change. Your Egoic Mind may bark orders and push for change ASAP, but, you do not have to listen to this voice. Flow and ease are elements of Oneness. Flow brings change over time at the right time—divine time. When we listen to the Egoic Mind when it pushes us to take drastic steps quickly in our lives, we make things harder for ourselves. The Egoic Mind may push us to change jobs, partners, homes quickly, but there is no need for the rushed energy of the Egoic Mind. When we give it up to God and ask what They want, over time we hear an answer that resonates with us and natural shifts begin to occur from remaining in the flow and ease of Oneness.

Holding Oneness shifted everything in my life within one year. The flow of Oneness was my teacher. It showed me that I was not taking responsibility for my life. I was not taking action on the callings within my heart. I was allowing others to treat me poorly, which taught them that their behavior was okay, and thus this cycle of demonstrating poor behavior towards me continued. At the time, I didn't know I could teach people how to love and treat me. I didn't know how to speak my truth, and didn't believe in myself which allowed others to tell me what was right for my life. As I followed other people's recommendations for my life instead of following my intuition, I watched as the person I used to be faded away. I watched as my spirit broke.

Some of you know how to take responsibility for your life and I'm so proud of you! There may be others like me who need insight into how this all works. If that's you, I want you to commit to working with an excellent therapist to understand what it is to take ownership of your life, to listen to yourself instead of others, and learn to be direct and speak your truth. Even when it's uncomfortable. As you gradually take back control of your life, this time you get to build your life the way you want it to be. Friend, you can be living the life you always dreamed of. That's what God wants for you—to be living the life you dream of.

SPIRIT WILL SHAKE YOU TO AWAKEN YOU

When I began holding Oneness, my dad had just passed away and I was working in a corporate job I loved, but was surrounded by people I did not resonate with. I was married to a man I loved, but our relationship was in a bad place. I am not a skilled cook; my idea of cooking is the crockpot. I don't clean, like ever—I organize, (but I now know cleaning and organizing are two different things).

My husband was born with OCD and is very particular about how everything should be done. I was born with ADHD and do not care at all how something gets done, or whether it gets done at all. This created a disconnect in our marriage where, for a time, all I heard were his criticisms.

- ⌘ "I don't like that music."
- ⌘ "You're not loading the dishwasher right."
- ⌘ "Don't turn the lights on that bright."
- ⌘ "Turn the TV volume down, it's too high!"
- ⌘ "Don't use the crockpot. I don't like soggy food."
- ⌘ "You're not vacuuming the corners of the room."
- ⌘ "Why are you taking a picture of that?"

And on, and on, and on. I felt small, unheard, and invisible most times. I changed who I was and walked on eggshells in hopes of not hearing more criticisms. I didn't know it at the time, but my husband felt like he was doing it all, and he was doing way more than his share. He was doing most of the cooking, cleaning, laundry, bills, and home maintenance. He was frustrated and needed my help. Neither of us knew how to speak to one another, hear one another out, or validate the other and move forward. Our frustrations with one another, combined with a lack of knowledge on how to communicate, led to a deep divide between us.

Have you ever heard the saying, "Spirit will shake you to awaken you?" Well, that's what ended up happening to me.

At the time, I didn't know what it was to take responsibility for my life and my actions, but I soon would!

I would sit in my work office dreaming of a new life. I did not know what an energy healer was at the time, so when I kept having a vision of myself working one-on-one with people, I thought what I was seeing was life coaching. Everytime I would daydream about this new life, my Egoic Mind would stop me and say, "That's not possible. You're making great money, you have the title you've always wanted and a team working for you. You're on a trajectory to the top of an amazing career. How could you even think about giving this up? Find a way to be happy here, in this role." When I found the courage to speak to my family about this, each person echoed my Egoic Mind.

I felt stuck with no way out.

At work, my ADHD conflicted with the way my boss wanted things done. She asked for 20-page write-ups detailing every small facet of my work. Each time I submitted my work for one assignment, she would toss it back to me only to ask for something entirely different. For the first time in my life, it felt like a supervisor and I weren't speaking the same language. The disconnect between my boss and I grew and grew. I prided myself on being a star employee at every job I worked, and was determined not to let that slip away. It was the one thing I felt I could control. So I began working around the clock, on days, nights, and weekends. I did this for two months, during which time, I barely saw my family or took time for myself.

I vividly remember my boss stopping by my office on a Friday night. It was 6:30pm, and as I stood packing up my things, she said, "Well, all weeks can't be winners!" I had been proud of my work that week. I knew I had done a great job, but having worked around the clock only for her to deliver those words to me, broke my spirit. I was crushed. I felt that if I were to bring my feelings to my husband, he would give me a look of disappointment and ask me to simply, "tough it out."

A thought came rushing in, "I don't want to be here anymore." I didn't mean my office—I meant my life. There was no way out. My Egoic Mind would say, "You know now what it is like to be on the Other Side. Your dad's shown you what it's like to be in Heaven. Why don't you just go there?"

My Egoic Mind wouldn't leave me alone about it, and soon the thought in my head changed from, "I don't want to be here anymore" to "I don't want to live anymore." I attached to the thought. I believed the thought, and fed my Egoic Mind more thoughts; "You're right, I don't want to be here anymore. I am stuck. There is no way out."

Looking back, I see now that we can never be stuck in life. We can be in situations that we don't want to be in, but at any moment we have the right, power and the ability to stand up for ourselves.

I had the freedom at any time to walk away from that job. I had the freedom to communicate loudly and firmly with my husband that I could not be in that job for one more day, and that I would no longer tolerate his criticisms. But I didn't do that.

With Oneness, we can step back and see any situation from God's perspective.

If I had, I would've seen that my boss was under severe pressure at the time. I would've honored that our personalities were like oil and vinegar: instead of seeing myself as "bad" or "wrong," I would've accepted the fact that we just did not mix well together. The truth was (and still is) that her view of me had nothing to do with me. Her view of me didn't make me bad or wrong, and it certainly didn't take away from my success or achievements! Had I accepted that, I would not have put such intense pressure on myself to change who I am. I would've simply left the job and found a new one where I was valued.

I could've also stepped back to be the observer of my marriage.

As an observer, I would've seen that not helping around the house (like at all) means hours more work on my husband and that was not an equal partnership. I would've seen that I wasn't taking responsibility for my part and that, too, was straining our partnership. Hindsight is 20/20, right?

At the time, I didn't see any of this. Blaming others was easier than taking responsibility for my part and role. My Egoic Mind pulled me onto a fast-moving train of negative thoughts. It told me I was stuck and there was no way out. Wrongly, I believed it.

From the time I first experienced suicidal ideation, to the moment I seriously contemplated taking my own life was just three weeks. That's how fast those thoughts can spiral.

Why am I telling you all of this? First, if you ever have suicidal thoughts, you must seek help for yourself immediately. God, your intuition, the Other Side, they will never give you any negative information. They will never tell you to harm yourself or anyone else in any way, shape or form. If you ever feel this down or have these thoughts you must go to a local hospital and work with a therapist to learn tools that can help you change your life. Spiritual tools will open up your connection with God and the Other Side, teach you how to trust your heart and work with your Angels, but therapy can help you understand how your brain works and how to repair relationships in your life. Spiritual work on yourself and therapy work beautifully in conjunction with one another. If you had to prioritize one, therapy always comes first. A great therapist will teach you to take responsibility and that only you hold the key to positive change within your own life.

That's the part I was missing back then. I was waiting for God to save me. I was waiting for my husband to one day magically change and hold me on a pedestal. I was waiting for my boss to magically change and see what an all-star I was. Holding Oneness while being around them allowed me to feel that something was off, but Oneness alone didn't give me the tools I needed to see my part, speak to them, and take action steps to change my life. That's why we need Earth angels like therapists!

My story changed when I told a coworker about my suicidal thoughts and she drove me to the hospital. The therapists I worked with in and outside of the hospital taught me how to see myself as an all-star and put myself on a pedestal. When I learned how to respect and love myself, no one outside of me could take that away; from that place, I could teach others how to treat me. By working with spiritual teachers and my therapists, I was able to rebuild my Spirit and rebuild my life according to the vision I had for myself, based on the callings of my heart.

As I did this work, Oneness taught me to see with love and honor that my life was not the only life that was challenging. Both my boss and my husband were going through their individual challenges. In the moment, it is easy for our Egoic Minds to make it about us exclusively, but when I looked back at the bigger picture, I saw how little I helped my husband. When I started helping, I was shocked at how much time simple, little tasks can take. I felt for the part of him that was shouting internally for help from me for so many years. He wanted to rest too. I felt for my boss as well, who was under extreme pressure at the time. She needed someone to do as she asked, which could have helped take the pressure off.

Learning to get into and hold Oneness does not and cannot cause issues in our lives.

Oneness cannot cause you to leave your job or have marital difficulties. Oneness is the state where all is well and healthy. It is simply that when you are in Oneness, your sense of which pieces of your life are and are not in alignment becomes keener, sharper. We do not throw out the parts of our lives that are not in alignment. We do the work to understand why these parts of our lives are not fully healthy. We can then do the work to get healthy (mentally, physically, emotionally and spiritually) and bring them up to a higher frequency so that we are in alignment with them. Once again, this requires spiritual, mental, emotional and physical help. It requires you to build and surround yourself with an Earthbound Spirit Team.

COUNSELORS: ONE SIZE DOES NOT FIT ALL

Friend, I believe that each of us needs to build an Earthbound Spirit Team of people who can help us in this lifetime. At the end of this book, you will create your own Earthbound Spirit Team, but here's what you need to know now: I've always included a therapist/counselor on my team. I believe that it is important to find the right counselor or therapist. Years before the previous story, my husband and I went to a female counselor who told my husband that all our marital issues were because of my ADHD—that if it weren't for that, we'd be fine. She never counseled him on his criticism of me or taught me how to work with my ADHD. My husband would later admit that he went to the next counselor with me (who we found after I broke) fully expecting this male counselor to say the same thing as the first: that our issues were due entirely to my ADHD. This new counselor didn't say that, because it simply wasn't true. Because this counselor was willing to dig a little deeper into the full scope of our layered issues, we were finally able to get the help we needed.

This is important because the right or wrong counselor is vital to your journey.

Today, I believe in interviewing different counselors before selecting the one for me. I pay them for their time by having an initial appointment where I can ask them questions I have about how they are trained and what tools they use. Some counselors have asked me to fill out a 5-to-10 page form detailing every aspect of my life before our first meeting. This form takes a lot of energy. I don't fill it out. I'm happy to later on, but only after I interview them first and select the counselor I want to work with.

When vetting different counselors, I ask them these four questions:

1. ***Do you specialize in understanding the brain, how it works, and how the brain impacts behavior?*** What training do you have in this? Sadly many counselors are only trained in how childhood impacts adulthood, yet it is the brain that drives so much of behavior. Many counselors have told me they did not take one course in how the brain works in order to obtain their college degree. When we understand how our loved ones' brains work, we can understand them and connect with them on a much deeper level. Yet, many therapists say they receive little to no training in this. This background knowledge in the brain is a must for me!

2. ***What do you do to continue learning and growing?*** If the response is, "I went to college for this," I'd politely leave! You want someone who is going to continue learning and growing so that they have the most innovative tools and methods to help you on your journey. Respectfully, I don't care how Freud did things, I want to know what is working for people today based on the latest research.

3. ***Do you find yourself appeasing and agreeing with clients instead of challenging them to grow?*** You don't need someone who's only going to affirm you all day. A counselor who's going to challenge you to look at your life from different perspectives and who's going to give you new tools to learn and grow is the key.

4. ***"What tools do you use to encourage couples to grow together?"*** (In the case of vetting a marital therapist or general therapist) I also ask, "Do you believe ADHD alone can be the reason a marriage doesn't work?" This can help gauge if they're going to truly encourage you and dig into the layered work of your relationships and if so, how?

Think of these questions as tools to help you determine which counselor can best help you grow, and can give you time with them to see if you resonate with their energy. I encourage you to add other questions you may have to this list, should you begin your own search for a counselor to work with!

ONENESS IN EVERYDAY LIFE

Friend, I'm so proud of you! You did it! You've spent an entire month learning how to hold and feel Oneness. You've learned to incorporate Oneness into your relationships by holding the energy in conversations. You've also learned to incorporate this energy more deeply into your everyday life!

You should be proud of yourself too!

Continue holding Oneness more and more in your life. One year from now, you will be shocked at how far you've come! As you flow through the year, try different Oneness routines (or spiritual practices) to see what works best for you. I still love waking up, taking one minute to tune my energy to Oneness, talking to God and then going about my day. I allow Oneness to be with me, and I keep my attention on it as I flow through my day, checking in with God and my Angels at lunch and again before bed. Oneness, in combination with this consistent communication with the Other Side, allows me to live in a beautiful flow of divine wisdom where I feel guided every step of the way!

Take some time to reflect on Oneness. What parts of your life are in alignment? These are areas of your life where everything feels good and is running smoothly.

_____

_____

_____

_____

_____

_____

_____

_____

_____

What areas of your life feel out of alignment? Remember these areas are not bad and you are not bad because of them. This is simply a way to become more aware of where you feel "out of alignment."

_____

_____

_____

_____

_____

_____

_____

_____

_____

How are you going to continue to make Oneness a priority in your life? What routines have worked well for you so far to get into and hold Oneness? Are there other routines that you'd like to try? Note those here and add anything else you want to remember about Oneness.

_____

_____

_____

_____

_____

_____

_____

_____

FROM ONENESS TO ANGEL COMMUNICATION

Friend, you're ready for the next step in your spiritual awakening: getting to know your angels!

When you go to a party, who is it easier to talk to? A friend you know or a stranger you've never met? A friend, right? It's the same when it comes to your angels. Many feel they should be able to hear from their angels the very first time they communicate with them. However, knowing your angels and building a relationship with them helps you form the strongest line of communication.

The first step in communicating with your angels is understanding:

⌘ Who they are

⌘ What their personalities are like

⌘ What they look like

⌘ How they make their presence known to you

⌘ What role they play in your life

⌘ How they've worked with you in the past

⌘ How they're working with you right now

When you apply too much pressure on yourself to hear your messages before you even know who your angels are and how they're working with you, it's the same as asking for directions in a country where you don't speak the language. You'd receive those directions in a foreign language and become frustrated that you cannot understand.

It's easier to work with your angels when you've taken the time to get to know them first.

For example, let's say Archangel Gabrielle is working on getting you to better communicate with your spouse by helping you utilize your throat chakra and speak your truth. You may begin to notice that when she's near, she shows you butterflies. One day you feel a dense, rock-like energy in your throat chakra, you keep seeing butterflies, and feeling Gabrielle's presence. Using your inner voice, you say, "I know you're with me Archangel Gabrielle. What would you have me know?" Because you recognize her signs and the sensations you feel in your body when she's in your presence, you understand her and it becomes much easier to communicate and receive her messages. Whereas, if you didn't take the time to learn about her, you might spend your day wondering why you're having this feeling in your throat.

Friend, do not discount the importance of getting to know your angels before you communicate with them!

The best way to use the following chapters on Angel Communication is to go through them twice: first, reading to simply get to know who your angels are, and reading a second time to go back through the Angel Communication chapters, practicing the journal prompts, and hearing, seeing, feeling, and knowing your angels' messages for your own life.

You've got this, friend! Let's dive in!

ANGEL COMMUNICATION

How to hear, see, feel, and talk to your angels!

A TWO-MONTH COURSE IN THE ANGEL MEMBERSHIP

Angel Communication is one course broken down into two parts:

Angel Communication Part 1 (four weeks)
and
Angel Communication Part 2 (four weeks).

ANGEL COMMUNICATION

Part 1: Week One

If you're in the Angel Membership,

go to the Angel Communication Part 1 course
(in the folder titled *A Year With Your Angels*):

☐ Watch **Teaching Video One.**

ANGELS SURROUND YOU

Surrounding you on every side are angels, extensions of God's loving energy sent to lift you up, nudge you forward, and keep you connected to your soul, Oneness, and God. The angels say, God sends more angels to surround you than there are cells within your body.

Friend, that's more than 37.2 trillion angels surrounding you right now.

Imagine yourself standing in a wide open space. Around you are over 37.2 trillion angels, forming multiple circles. Each one of them is sending you love and holding open the portal to Oneness (your angels call it "Home energy") for you to tap into and feel at any time. Pause to tap into this energy. What does it feel like when 37.2 trillion angels send you love at the same time? When I do this exercise, I feel a love so great that joy-filled tears stream down my face. God's love, the love of our angels, is so much more than we know it to be.

Each of your 37.2 trillion angels knows your name, they know who you are in the eyes of God and why your soul is here on Earth out of the infinite number of souls who could be. Your angels knew you in Heaven before you chose to come to Earth. They know every facet of your personality, every pain you've ever endured (in this lifetime or any other). Your angels know what brings you joy, how to bring out the best in you, and the path to your best life here.

Beautiful soul, you don't know how special you are in the eyes of God and your angels. To them, you are everything. You represent the Oneness of All That Is. To them, you *are* all that is.

If you are reading this book, you must understand that your angels guided you to it because there are messages here that can better clarify certain things on your path.

Friend, having access to over 37.2 trillion angels whose mission it is to help you in every area of your life is like having the most intuitive technology in the multiverse. Until now, you haven't been utilizing the power of your angels and the magnitude of heavy lifting they want to do in your life. You've been walking this life journey alone, assuming you had to do it by yourself. Through your angels, you have every answer to every life challenge big or small. Through your angels, you have a direct connection to God, God's will for your life, God's knowledge of you, and divine wisdom of everything everywhere.

In the following chapters, your Spirit Team and I will teach you how to:

⌘ be in communication with your angels always

⌘ hear the words angels whisper in your ears

⌘ see the visions your angels place within your third eye/imagination

⌘ feel and know the messages your angels bring to you

My students find it best to go through this material twice. First, go through and simply read about each angel to get a better understanding of who they are and how they're working with you. Once you get to know your angels, you'll find it easier to go back through the material a second time around and try the Automatic Writing prompts. If you need help, the Angel Membership's Angel Communication course is the best resource to help you more deeply grasp this material. In the Angel Membership this course is broken down into two parts lasting four weeks each: Angel Communication Part 1 and Angel Communication Part 2.

Friend, your angels are standing next to you as you read this!

Say a little prayer to God and ask for your angels' guidance as you read the following chapters. They whisper to you, "Open your heart to all of the miracles and blessings that are on their way to you right now. You can feel our presence and hear our messages. All you have to do is remain open and believe."

Get ready! Your angels are about to work wonders in your life!

WHAT ARE ANGELS?

Angels are selfless beings and the question, "What are angels?" has more to do with who God is and who you are, than angels themselves. Let's start with who God is.

God is All That Is, all energy everywhere. We know two things about God: God is both creator and being. You are one droplet in the ocean that is God and because that droplet can never be separate from the ocean, you are one with God. Your soul is made in the likeness and image of God in that you, too, are both creator and being. You've probably heard the sayings before: "We are not human beings having a spiritual experience. We are spiritual beings having a human experience." (Pierre Teilhard de Chardin). "God dwells within you, as you. God is not interested in watching a performance of how a spiritual person behaves. God dwells within me, as me" (Elizabeth Gilbert, *Eat, Pray, Love*).

You are here on purpose. You are not here to fake your way through life by appeasing everyone around you. You are here to be you. You are here to both embody and express love, joy, peace, bliss, ease, and grace. You are here to live out the desires that call to you within your heart and come back to a remembrance that you are "creator." You are here to create and be that which serves humanity and your own heart simultaneously.

So, what blocks you from being who you are? Your own individual Egoic Mind and the Egoic Mind of the collective consciousness. This is where your angels come in, because this is their purpose.

Angels are extensions of God's energy. The only way for you to truly understand this is to see it within your imagination and feel it within your heart. Visualize this, God is All That Is. Imagine in every direction all multiverses, every planet, star, and realm everywhere—God is all of it. God is able to allow a dream-like state on Earth through the tool that is the Egoic Mind. The Egoic Mind is not truth; it is not God, but it is allowed by God as a tool, by which parts of God (souls) can experience itself. As souls on Earth, we experience the love, joy, peace, bliss, ease, and grace that we truly are through living our lives.

In order to experience these parts of ourselves, we must forget who we are as souls at birth. We live with amnesia, never fully remembering our existence before this life. As souls on Earth, we seek God because this place never feels completely right, never feels fully like "home." Intuitively, we know there is much more to the story than we've been told (and we're right)!

Awakening is remembering who we are as souls: remembering God didn't send us on this journey alone; that we are phenomenal creators and the power (freewill) lies within us to take action in this lifetime in order to create the lives and changes we want to see. Friend, the truth of the matter is that God doesn't allow us to stray far from Them. The truth is, God stacked the deck in our favor by giving us angels.

God created angels as extensions of Their energy to ensure we don't forget who we are. I've heard people say if God were the sun, Angels are rays of the sun's energy extending out in every direction (the angels love this analogy and say it's spot on). Listen, this might be a controversial thing to say, but as a mother myself I've often thought that if I could implant a chip into my kiddo and know where she was at every moment in order to keep her safe in life, I absolutely would. That's what God did with us! God equipped us with angels to help us in every way in this lifetime, not only to protect us but to keep us connected, and make this life fun and joyful, and to give us an edge over the Egoic Mind. If you allow them to:

⌘ There is no way for you to be lost from God for forever—your angels will always guide you back home.

⌘ There is no way for you not to feel God's energy, Oneness, the vibration of your soul—your angels are always holding the portal door open to Oneness for you to get into at any time.

⌘ There is no way for you not to meet the life partner, family, and friends that you are to share this life with—your angels know every freewill choice that will be made, they know everything that is to come, and they are able to impress upon your heart where you need to be at a precise time.

⌘ There is no way for you not to fulfill your life's purpose here—your angels know you better than you know yourself. They know exactly why you are here and they help you unfold into a better understanding of yourself throughout your whole life.

⌘ There is no way for you not to experience profound joy here on Earth—your angels know your soul, what makes you, you and they encourage you to make living your life fun!

The only thing stopping you from living life this way is your Egoic Mind and the Egoic Mind of the collective consciousness. Angels are not fighting some big battle in the sky, but they do fight battles within your mind every day.

Working with your angels changes everything! When you know how to hear, see, feel, and know your angels' presence and the messages they deliver to you in your own life, it gives you the peace and confidence to know that every single moment of your life is guided. You release control, you surrender to the flow and joys of life, and you take bold action steps forward, as you watch in awe at the miracles unfolding, as the ideas within your heart manifest into your reality. You begin to see yourself as "co-creator" as God helps you build "out of thin air" the desires of your heart, the purpose of your soul. This is the purpose of your angels, to help you step into the authority God gave you—to help you be fully and authentically you.

ONENESS IS THE KEY

To Working With Your Angels

If you've skipped the chapters on Oneness because you're excited to work with your angels, you need to know that Oneness is the tool used to make the connection with your angels. You can't watch a TV show without a TV or device to watch it on. You can't hear the radio DJ without a radio or device to listen on. In the same way, Oneness is the energetic device you use to hear, see, feel, and know your angels' messages. Oneness is like a radio or phone line between you and the Other Side. In order to fully learn how to connect with your angels, you must know how to get into and hold the state of Oneness. In doing so, you're holding the phone line open between you and Heaven.

When you get into and hold Oneness, all of your 37.2 trillion cells and the over 37.2 trillion molecules surrounding you within your auric field are all open connecting your energy here on Earth to God-energy on the Other Side. When you're in Oneness you know it. It's palpable. You feel tingly, your energy feels expansive in all directions, you feel present and consciously aware of what's happening with you now. In Oneness, the volume of your Egoic Mind turns down and the volume of your intuition (soul's voice) turns up. Your intuition is the phone receiver and how you hear your angels more clearly. If you haven't learned to get into and hold a state of Oneness, please go back to read the previous chapters. Once you've finished Oneness, you'll be ready to dive in and connect with your angels more easily.

BELIEF IS A FREEWILL CHOICE

Next to Oneness, your openness, faith, trust and belief is the second most important tool you have in connecting with your angels. Your angels say you get what you believe. If you have faith, trust, and believe that you will be able to connect with your angels, you will connect. If you lack faith and doubt your abilities to connect with your angels, you will struggle.

Your angels need you to know that struggle is *not* necessary.

Discard that struggle right now! Instead, see all of your angels circling around you. They hold the palms of their hands up towards your heart and they ask you, "May we remove any doubt energy within your body, chakras, and auric field?" If you say yes, feel within your mind, heart, and entire physical body that they are now removing any fear and doubt energy. I want you to feel your body becoming lighter and more airy, almost like you could float. Your angels ask you to imagine yourself one month from now talking to someone about this book and the Angel Membership program. You say to this person, "I'm so excited I could cry! I've been working on connecting with my angels and receiving their messages all month, and I got it! I did it! I can talk to them and hear their messages for my life! I'm so excited because I know I will use this tool my entire life to communicate with my Spirit Team!"

Friend, if you feel doubt creeping in at any time I want you to come back to this exercise and do it again. Use this as a tool whenever you need it to overcome your negative thoughts.

GET TO KNOW YOUR ANGELS

Over the course of the next two months, you're going to get to know your angels well. The information that I've channeled through might be different from that of other messengers and that's alright! I am an energy healer and can feel into different angelic energies. I also have the gift of hearing my angels, and seeing visions or messages that the angels place within my mind's eye (imagination). This month, I want you to read the material on each angel as I've presented it and then spend time with that angel, getting to know them better for yourself.

Here's what you need to know to get started. Each angel has their own personality and role they play in your life. I view my angels as extensions of my family and I feel the personalities/energy of my angels, just like I feel the personalities/energy of different family members.

My mom has a very fun-loving personality. She smiles all the time, and when I think of her, I can immediately feel what it's like to hold her hand and how soft her skin is. She feels like home and unconditional love.

My mom's energy and personality is much different from my husband's. His energy also feels like home and unconditional love, but with him I also feel unconditional support. No matter what I do or say, or how I grow, he's always got my back. Not in a peppy cheerleader type of way, but in a protective way that brings me a deep sense of peace, love, safety, and security. It's a support like none I've ever felt in my life before. It's a support that has given me the courage to take action on the callings within my heart and do so much more than I ever could've dreamed.

My mom and husband's energy is vastly different from my best friend's energy. Sarah's been my cheerleader since we were 19 and (I hope) I am hers. I called her when I was thinking of starting a foundation for kids born with the same syndrome as my daughter's. She jumped into action. She had her husband create a logo and she came with me to California to learn the in's and out's of starting a non profit organization. She's the one I called when I was thinking of starting a podcast years ago. I called and said, "So I have this idea but I don't know anything about podcasts, and I'm scared to do this." Out of nowhere she goes, "Julie, I listen to about 4–6 hours of podcasts each day. I'll teach you everything." And she did! She showed up at my birthday dinner the next year with my podcast image plastered on a mug and bag. Her enthusiasm and positivity has gotten me through moments of my life where I was sure life was going to break me!

Each of the people above plays an extremely special role in my life. I need each of them, and I look to them for support in different ways. You have the same support in your life; people with vastly different personalities who play different roles. You benefit from the combined support of each of your relationships with them, and it is the same way with your angels.

Getting to know your angels is getting to know their different personalities and the varying roles they play in your life. By understanding these roles you'll begin to see how angels are working with you now and you'll learn to see the messages they share with you for your life.

This is the point in the book where many authors would talk to you about the levels or choirs of angels, but the angels want you to know that there is no true hierarchy of angels: just as your body functions as a cohesive unit (brain, heart, bones, skin, organs, neural networks), all angels function as a cohesive unit as well, regardless of their "choir" status. Focus on getting to know each of the angels' personalities and the roles they play in your life.

Right now, you probably have a million questions! As we examine each of the angels individually, you will gradually understand how the Cherubs, Seraphim, Archangels and Guardian angels are all working with you simultaneously. You'll better understand angel numbers, angel signs and use them to distinguish who is working with you.

Friend, it's time for you to do the work and begin getting to know your angels! Let's go!

CAN I TALK TO ANGELS?

When you're getting to know your angels, many people ask if you can talk directly to them or if you must only talk to God. People have very strong and mixed beliefs on whether or not we should even be talking to angels. Some say that we must go directly to God. I've spoken to God about this and They told me not to be concerned about talking to angels or what others have to say about it. We must normalize talking to God's angels. God says that angels are an extension of Their energy. While we human souls will always have some form of an Egoic Mind in this lifetime, angels do not. Angels are God's energy in action.

God says that if you are concerned about this you can either:

1. Keep your communication directly between you and God.

2. Or you can ask God to only allow you to connect to Their energy and any beings (angels, loved ones in Heaven, or guides) that stand in God's energy.

If you use the latter, you can say the following prayer and release any fear energy within you. Fear is not of God, it is a product of the Egoic Mind. If you've prayed this prayer, you've made your intentions known to God and They will protect you.

> *Dear God,*
>
> *It is my wish that you work through me in this lifetime. Please help me, guide me, direct me and protect me at every moment. God, now and always, please only allow me to connect to angels, guides and loved ones who stand in your energy and do your will. Throughout my entire lifetime, please let me hear your voice loudly and clearly God, through all beings that do your will.*
>
> *Amen*

AUTOMATIC WRITING 101

After this section, you will explore information I've channeled on 17 angels. You will focus on a few different angels each week. After reading about each one, I want you to connect with that angel through Automatic Writing for 10–15 minutes. Automatic Writing is the same as prayer. When you pray, you get quiet with God and can ask Them questions. Those questions are answered in divine time. The difference with Automatic Writing is that it is written down. It is simply a form of communication between you, God, your angels, and loved ones on the Other Side.

Some assume that Automatic Writing is allowing your pen to move around the page making beautiful art, but this is not the Automatic Writing I'm referring to. I mean that you ask your angels a question and write down words and sentences exactly as they come to you.

It is the tool you will use to build a relationship with your angels so that you hear, see, feel, and know them more clearly.

There is a process to Automatic Writing. You will need a pen and paper or a computer to type. When you try Automatic Writing with your angels, here are the steps you'll want to take:

1. First, read about the angel you are studying and focusing on.

2. Next, get into a state of Oneness because from that vibration your energy is dialed into the radio frequency of the Other Side. Oneness connects you and puts you in an aligned vibration with the Other Side.

3. Use your imagination to see the angel you wish to connect with and ask them to spend time with you.

4. Ask your angel a question. I've provided journal prompts for you for each angel. Then sit in Oneness and allow the answer to come to you through your own internal dialogue. Your angels will not sound like a voice outside of you, they will use your own internal dialogue voice to communicate to you.

5. Do not second guess what comes to you. The first answer you receive is what to write down verbatim.

6. Do not try and mentally process what you are writing as you are writing it. It is extremely difficult to mentally process what you're writing and continue to write at the same time. Just allow the words to flow through your pen until you get to the point where there are no more words, and you are done.

7. When the information has stopped pouring through, you can go back to read and process what you wrote. Oftentimes, you'll find that what you write sounds a bit different from how you would've written it yourself. This is one way of knowing it's angels and not you.

As you try Automatic Writing, your Egoic Mind is going to come in and say things like, "Is this real? Am I just making this up? How do I know it's my angels and not just me writing this?" Friend, it's not bad to have these thoughts, it means you're human! There are, however, a few ways to work through it.

First, ask your angels for signs or validation. Say to each angel you work with, "Please show me a sign or validate my Automatic Writing experience today so that I know without a doubt that it is truly you coming through with messages for me." Your angel will give you a sign, symbol, or color you can use to validate it is them, each time. Friend, in order to receive signs, you must believe that they will be shown to you.

Most people get the hang of Automatic Writing within the first two weeks, although I've worked with the rare student or two who practiced every day for two months before the words really began to flow. If you feel like the words are not coming, or they are not coming as quickly as you want them to, be patient. Your angels say that you will either begin this journey and work through this now, or become frustrated, wait five years and pick it up again then, wishing you hadn't given up the first time. Whatever you do, don't give up! Practice every day if you can, and you will find that the words will indeed come to you.

Some people ask, "Julie, in order to do Automatic Writing you must be able to hear from the angels. What if 'hearing' is not one of my gifts?" Friend, many people place too much emphasis on the "four Clairs" (*clairaudience*, hearing; *clairsentience*, feeling; *clairvoyance*, seeing; and *claircognizance*, knowing) without realizing we have all of them at once.

The angels say that developing these gifts and using them to help others is called giving a "reading" because it is similar to reading a book. When you read, you use your eyes to scan the words on the page, but at the same time you are speaking those words to yourself and hearing them with your own internal dialogue (clairaudience). You may read something descriptive in the book and see a picture within your imagination (clairvoyance). A character may get hurt or pass away in the book and you will feel the energy through your own emotions or physical body (clairsentience). You may have a knowingness, "Oh my goodness, this is what's going to happen in the book (claircognizance)!" When you read, you use all four Clairs, and this is the same thing in your everyday life!

The angels want you to know that you have the ability to hear them and build a relationship with them through Automatic Writing for the purpose of you bringing through messages for yourself in your own life. Remember, there is much more that goes into bringing through messages for other people and being an angel messenger or angel reiki healer. You can be held accountable for doing this work as a profession without any training. What I need you to know is that learning to connect with your angels for your own personal growth is much different from training to bring through messages for other people.

The joy of learning to communicate with your angels for yourself is learning how to live your life with more ease, grace, love, and bliss by working one-on-one with them every day!

I want you to concentrate on one angel a day instead of trying to work with multiple angels each day, this way you'll get a better understanding of what their energy is like. When you work with multiple angels a day (at the beginning), it's like a party where you end up confusing their energies because you don't understand who is talking when. Instead, working with one angel a day, allows you to immerse yourself in that particular angel's energy and truly get to know them. That angel will be working with you throughout your day and you may find yourself coming back to your Automatic Writing paper to jot things down as your day progresses.

Before you dive in, I want you to know: getting to know your angels over the next two months and deeply working with them to heal spiritually are two separate things. You wouldn't go into a counselor's office expecting to be done after one visit, nor would you expect that when you get married, you just show up to the big day and everything is magically ready to go without any advanced preparation. There can be years of work that go into planning a wedding, and the same goes for working with your angels. You cannot expect to know everything about connecting with your angels by working with them one day or over the course of two months. By doing this work you're committing to a practice of including your angels in your everyday life for the rest of your entire life.

It is a relationship you are building with each of your angels over time and it all starts here!

You will make huge strides over the next two months! By the end of this book you'll know all the major players on your Spirit Team and how to communicate with them.

Remember, your angels will never bring through any negative information. They will not tell you to harm yourself or anyone else or anything else. The angels and any being connected to God will only bring through positive, loving messages. It is important for you to understand that any negative information is from the Egoic Mind. Also, please use discernment when it comes to the messages you get for yourself. For example, when I first started doing this work, I could see myself working as a full time entrepreneur. However, I also needed to contribute to my monthly household bills as I was building a new business. My angels led me to a way to do both. I got a part time gig that allowed me to pay the bills and start my business. I need you to see that while I am teaching you to bring through messages for yourself, only you (and you alone) can make your decisions for your life. Choose what is best for you and your family in your life always!

Alright! It's time for you to begin communicating with your angels one-by-one. Continue to work through this book focusing on one angel at a time, over the next two months. I'll touch on information about your Spirit Team, how to build angel teams, and (briefly) how you can connect with your loved ones on the Other Side!

If you're worried that you'll get it wrong or won't be able to connect with your angels, they want to reassure you that that's not possible. It is your birthright to work with them because your angels are extensions of God. They remind you that nothing can stop you from connecting with them but your fear. Take a moment to say this prayer:

> *Dear God,*
>
> *Please remove any fear within me and show me a glimpse of my future where I am able to hear, see, feel and know the messages my angels have for me in my everyday life. Instill within me a confidence and a knowing that I am able to easily connect with my angels at any time I need to, now and for the rest of my life.*
>
> *Amen*

ANGEL
COMMUNICATION
Part 1: Week Two

If you're in the Angel Membership,
go to the Angel Communication Part 1 course
(in the folder titled *A Year With Your Angels*):

☐ Watch **Q&A Video Recording One**.

☐ Listen to the prerecorded healing session
titled **Angel Reiki Energy Healing.**

GUARDIAN ANGELS

Out of an infinite number of angels, God selected your guardian angel or angels just for you. I see people rank angels all the time and want to work with their Archangels most, but your guardian angel was designed just for you and your life journey. Your guardian angel was designed to be your best friend; an unconditional, everlasting support, and constant connection to God.

You may have one, two, or three guardian angels with you your entire lifetime.

Your number of guardian angels depends on how you need to grow and serve in this lifetime, and what experiences you will move through. Accessing this information and what to call your guardian angels is easy. Get into a state of Oneness and ask God, "How many guardian angels do I have in this lifetime?" Wait to hear a number then ask, "What is the name of my first guardian angel?" Wait for the answer then ask about the second and third.

When you do this, note what thought comes to you first: do not second guess it. Believe the first thought that comes to you. If you do not hear anything at first, that's okay too. Simply pray about it then go about your day and your guardian angels' names will come to you in a flash "a-ha" moment. You might read something, or see a name on the internet and go, "That's it! That's my guardian angel's name. I know it is!"

I often find that people are so worried about getting the name of their guardian angel wrong, they often procrastinate on naming their angel for years. Spirit says we need to see this another way. God's primary language is not English, nor any other language on Earth. God's language is vibration. Why was it that when man went to God and said, "God, what is your name," God said "I am," because God's name cannot truly be described in an Earthly language, and neither can the names of Angels.

Words cannot describe the magnitude and awe of God or the angels, but giving them names can help us communicate with them and navigate this life better.

Select a name that resonates. Meaning, select a name that makes you feel Oneness. If you feel the name holds the vibration of Oneness, it's the perfect name! Naming your angels is important because you will be communicating with them often!

Your guardian angel loves you as if you were their child, mother, father, sibling, and best friend all in one. They know how all 37.2 trillion cells in your body operate, they know each of the 12,000–60,000 thoughts you have each day. They know exactly what you want and need in a partner and the career best suited for you. Because there is no time, they've seen what freewill decisions you will choose (and the choices of others). They know how every moment of your life will unfold (though telling you would bypass your freewill so they cannot and will not do that).

Your guardian angel knows you better than you know yourself. They were created to be everything you need in this life, and hold the answer to every question you could possibly ask. Their inherent presence is one of home, safety, security, comfort, joy, love, cheer, and every other positive emotion you need to feel in this lifetime.

At times, additional angel guides come in who serve like a guardian angel, but only for a period in our life. Every time we go through something major in our life, additional angels come in to support us. Like our guardian angels, these angels come in with a similar type of energy created to help us, specifically, with the big life event or challenge.

Do not presume that these angels only present themselves when something bad is about to happen. That is not the case. It's not about the life event being positive or negative, it's about how dense the energy is.

A wedding is a joyous occasion. However, anyone who's planned a wedding knows how stressful and anxiety-inducing it can be to make a million little decisions. Because you want that day to be absolutely perfect, there is an angel guide to support you in that event. In the same way, an angel guide comes in for every pregnancy, home purchase, decision on whether or not to move, take a new job, etc. If you are experiencing a big life event right now, or anticipate one coming up, you no doubt have an angel guide who is already assisting you!

Your guardian angel manages most of the 37.2+ trillion angels that work on your behalf. It seems impossible that there could really be that many angels working with you, but I assure it is true. Years ago a show came on (the name of which escapes me, now) and in the intro was a visual that showed lines of energy connecting each moment in our lives. It showed how the lines of our life's path intersect with the lines of other people's life paths.

The job of most of these 37.2 trillion angels is to know every line and thread of energy in your life and how those energetic lines intersect with those you know and don't know. For example, if you leave your house to run an errand at 10:02 you might miss someone you were to connect with, but if you leave the house at 10:04 you'll meet up with them in perfect timing. Keeping you on track and setting everything up in your life is not a simple task. Just as it takes 37.2+ trillion cells to make your body run, it takes the same (if not more) number of angels to continue propelling you forward in this life.

It's time for you to get to know your guardian angel(s)!

Get into a state of Oneness and pray, "God, how many Guardian Angels do I have that will be with me my whole life?" Allow the number to come to you and record it below. For each of your guardian angels, ask one-at-a-time, "What would you like to be called so that I can more easily communicate with you?" Ask God, "Do I have any additional angel guides helping me at this time in my life?" Keep track of this information below so that we can use it when talking about Angel Teams in week eight.

_____

_____

_____

_____

_____

_____

_____

_____

_____

_____

_____

_____

_____

_____

_____

_____

_____

ARCHANGEL MICHAEL

Remember being a kid and seeing a cartoon skit of a character with an angel on one side of their head and a devil on the other? In the cartoon skit, the character would be deliberating over a choice they needed to make, and the angel and devil were feeding them thoughts. "You should do this," one would say. "No, you should do this," the other would shout! Friend, despite his fierce appearance (always with a sword in his hand) Archangel Michael does not wage wars in the sky. The wars he wages are with your mind.

He is one of the angels on your shoulder feeding you positive, loving thoughts.

Archangel Michael is the angel responsible for helping you battle your Egoic-Minded thoughts by listening to your intuition. In doing this work, Archangel Michael helps you remain close to the voice of God, your Spirit Team, and your Higher Self. Friend, this is an enormous job. If there are 7.5 billion people on Earth and each has up to 60,000 thoughts a day, that means Archangel Michael manages the energy of over 450 trillion thoughts a day.

He doesn't do this alone.

Archangel Michael works directly with your guardian angel and most of the 37.2 trillion angels surrounding you in order to keep continual tabs on you, everything you're thinking and everything that's happening in your life. Through this network of angels, Archangel Michael helps you to be more aware of your thoughts; trust your intuition; heal your Inner Child; shift your thoughts and rewrite the stories within your mind; visualize a new future for yourself and take action to make that vision reality.

Your soul came here knowing it wanted to experience certain joys, learn, and grow through specific lessons, and serve humanity in some way. Together, these things form your life plan and the only thing that can block you from being on your path is the Egoic Mind (both within you and the collective consciousness). Archangel Michael's ultimate role is to keep you on your path and aligned with your soul plan by not allowing your Egoic Mind to block you, or hold you back by sabotaging your progress.

When you feel Archangel Michael's energy, it is massive. You can feel an expansion into All That Is. You may think of him as a warrior, but when I work with Archangel Michael he is the biggest teddy bear. The essence of his being is safety, security, and pure love. He radiates love constantly. When

Archangel Michael is around, you become more calm, you feel safe, secure, at peace, and loved. His presence is like a father scooping you up, hugging you tight, and (telepathically) telling you that everything is going to be okay.

Just as humans need food, water, and shelter to survive, Archangel Michael says we need love, safety, and security. Not only does he protect us from the Egoic Mind (in ourselves and the world), his presence is felt and his signs are seen by billions daily as he works to connect us to God's love and the safety and security God provides.

Archangel Michael works with every human on Earth. If you are going through a challenging time in your life, healing past emotional wounds, or suffer from anxiety or mental health challenges—Archangel Michael is working with you, and wants you to call on him every time you need support. Have you ever heard someone say not to call on angels because they are too busy handling the big stuff? Friend, this couldn't be further from the truth! People who say this are projecting our human capacities onto angels. Angels are not bound by the Egoic Mind and do not have the limitations of the physical body. They are able to do all, see all, and be all without ever tiring. In my sessions, Archangel Michael is constantly telling people, "Hand me all of your worries. I will manage all of them for you and replace their energy with peace inside your mind."

Remember that despite those who say, "Do not talk to your angels because you don't know who you're talking to. Only speak directly to God," all you have to do is pray to God one time:

> *Dear God,*
>
> *Please only ever allow me to connect to your energy God and any beings who walk in your energy for now and my entire life.*
>
> *Amen*

God is not trying to trick you or create crazy complex rules to confuse you. When you say this prayer once, know it is taken care of in your life. Become more comfortable talking to God or your angels because the only angels you'll be connecting with are extensions of God's energy. Remember, your angels never bring through any negative information. Your angels only bring through positive, loving information to help guide you, direct you, and protect you.

In the Angel Membership program, we work directly with Archangel Michael in the Healing Your Inner Child course.

Get into a state of Oneness. Ask Archangel Michael the following questions (always asking one question at a time). Pause and write the answers that flow to you.

1. Archangel Michael, how are you working with me in my life right now?

2. What are the top three Egoic-Minded thoughts you're helping me to release?

3. What would you like me to know to help me on my journey now?

4. Please show me a vision (or visions) of the future God has for me.

_____

_____

_____

_____

_____

_____

_____

_____

_____

_____

_____

_____

_____

_____

_____

_____

SARAPHINA AND THE SERAPHIM

In my very first practice session during my energy healing training, an angel appeared by my side and brought through information for my client. I asked her what her name was and she said, "Saraphina." (I've asked her about the spelling of her name, and she said some spell it with an "e," others with an "a" and both are acceptable). Saraphina has worked with me every day since, and is working with many of you. One of the first things that I noticed about Saraphina is that the shape of her wings are different. She does not have six wings as reported about other Seraphim angels, but the shape of her wings are different from Archangels. Her wings are longer and thinner, but just as full and beautifully radiant.

At first, I thought Saraphina to be an Archangel because she works so closely with Archangels Michael, Gabrielle, and Raphael. In fact, when you feel her energy, it is the female equivalent of Archangel Michael's energy, vast and massive.

Saraphina is not an archangel, she comes from the Seraphim order.

Saraphina is one of twelve Seraphim angels sent here to Earth, in 2011, for a specific mission. The Seraphim angels do not look the same to each person. When I see the 12 Seraphim angels, they are truly diverse, representing humans from around the world. The Seraphim angels come through to us in a way that allows our minds to comprehend their presence. Saraphina explained to me that the way angels are perceived and received by humans here on Earth has everything to do with us simply accepting and believing in their message—that is to say, people see them differently. The truth is their beauty is so magnificent and radiant, it would be hard for us to look at them with human eyes.

What the Seraphim angels need from us right now is to take action. If you are alive right now, you are living during one of the most important times in history to date. The advancements made between 1970–2020 are nothing in comparison to new advancements that will be made over the next fifty years. The Seraphim are here to help guide this transition and help guide the world to be a love-filled place of peace for all. The Seraphim say that in order to get to this place, our souls must wake up, remember the part they are here to play (from love, with love), and take action.

One day, when I first started this work some years ago, I was in a session with a stranger I had never met before. I was working with her energy on the massage table and the angels asked me to work on her back. I was shocked when, up near her shoulder blades, I could feel the energetic presence of wings. (Often, when I'm in a session, I feel something energetically first and then a vision will come into my mind clarifying what I've just felt). After I felt the wings, I immediately saw a vision of a place on the Other Side where souls have wings. When I tap into the Other Side, they show me many different places, but never before had I seen a place where souls had wings. Angels yes, but souls? No. I had never seen this before. It was a special group. I was in complete shock and had so many questions, and Saraphina was there to answer each one.

"Who is the group of souls on the Other Side and why do they have wings?" I asked, "Are they angels?"

"No, they are not angels like us. Angels have not lived lifetimes as souls in bodies, but these souls have lived many lifetimes."

The vision they were showing me of the Other Side became clearer. I saw a complete community of souls with diverse appearances on the Other Side. Like Saraphina, they were the most beautiful beings I'd ever seen. Their beauty transcended our Earthly perceptions and standards of beauty. The beauty of the Seraphim is felt, more like an emotion. Their beauty holds a grand essence of awe and wonder at our world. Believe it or not, the Seraphim angels are in awe of us!

Their beauty also holds a vision of our future. When we think about the future of this planet, we often feel fear of all the "what if's". The Seraphim do not feel fear. They hold space, and a vision within their consciousness of not just our survival, but of the human collective choosing to overcome all obstacles by doing the work, choosing love, choosing Oneness, and choosing to take action from Oneness. They are here to help us overcome and they have many helpers within humanity.

That day, I knew those wings in my client's back were the first I'd felt, but wouldn't be the last.

Since then, I've felt the energy of wings and the connectedness to the Seraphim in hundreds of clients. The Seraphim say this group is here because they were asked to come help the world make a transition to a loving, peace-filled society. These souls are human. They experience the wide range of human emotions. However, they have a deep and solid foundation within them that is not here to accumulate riches in this lifetime, or to be part of the old realm of society that falsely made perfection out to be "the norm." These souls are God's pure love, and put the needs of the collective before their own interests. They are not only able to hold Oneness, but are also here to take action as well. And they do! Some are activists, others are healers, or messengers. These souls have been called and strategically placed in every line of work on Earth.

Saraphina says to tell you that the chills or "ah-ha moment" you're experiencing right now is a remembrance of who you are and why you're here.

If you are experiencing this right now, you my friend are one of these winged souls!

The Seraphim are not only working with these winged-souls, but all healers on Earth. Remember, healers are in every line of work possible. In meditation one day in 2020, Saraphina came to me. She said, "There will be fourteen waves of healers in your lifetime. The third wave of healers is being ushered in right now." By ushered in, she means right now they are awakening to a vision within their mind or calling within their heart of the life they know they're truly here to live. She says that many feel fear and their Egoic Mind is telling them they are "late to the game." If that's you, please take a moment to say a prayer and ask God to release this energy from your heart.

Friend, you are not late. You are waking up right on time. Do not let fear hold you back from claiming the life you were sent here to live.

The Seraphim have a massive job which requires "all souls on deck." As technology accelerates, humanity changes at the most rapid rate in history, thus far. An opportunity lies ahead for a new Earth to be built. The direction of this new Earth and what it looks like is the responsibility of each soul, company, and organization. Each individual choice impacts the collective. The Seraphim are guiding humanity to usher in a new Earth that is free from the Egoic Mind, fear, and greed.

The Seraphim say that in order to usher in a new Earth, each individual must work through both their individual and collective ancestral trauma.

On both levels, ancestral trauma is energetic and cannot be perceived with the physical eye. Ancestral trauma is like energetic wounds that are still open and living within each human's DNA. It is rooted in fear and likes to repeat what it's done in the past, because that's all it knows. Therefore, in order to build a new Earth, it is the job of every soul to do the work to heal their own ancestral trauma.

When humans do their work, they are able to step out of the individual Egoic Mind, and unzipping a full-body costume off themselves and returning to the essence of their soul-self underneath. It's a state of Oneness, love, joy, peace, bliss, ease, and grace. The work it takes to get to this energetically healed place doesn't happen overnight. It takes time, consistent practice, and patience with ourselves to work through our "stuff."

The collective Egoic Mind will not shift on a large scale until enough humans (including those who lead governments, corporations, and organizations) all do continued work on themselves and the systemic structures of which they're a part. Doing the work is energetically carving out a new pathway for humanity. Together, as we do this work both individually and collectively, we are carving out and building the foundation for a new Earth. It is not easy or quick work, but this is necessary work that will shift and change our lives, the lives of others, and the world as we know it.

If you are a soul on Earth at this very moment, you have work to do! You are needed and so valuable. Your life holds deep, deep purpose. With that said, Saraphina wants you to know you cannot run this race 24/7, 365, nor can you change your entire life overnight. Your life is where it is at on purpose. You have been through experiences that have enabled you to help both individuals and the collective heal. However, the Seraphim acknowledge that it is equally important to care for yourself and enjoy this life. On the Other Side, you are a soul with limitless energy, but on the physical realm, you possess a human body that will tire if you don't care for it properly. Pushing yourself to change overnight or work endlessly (without rest, relaxation or experiencing the joys of life) will break you. The Seraphim say, "Please don't do this to yourself." Your angels are not asking you to work nonstop. All energy that pushes you to go and go without serious accomodation for your physical and mental wellbeing comes from the Egoic Mind.

As you do your work, your angels ask you to care for yourself and love yourself more. Only by living your joy, in Oneness, and by living a more balanced life will you be able to serve others and help create a new, peace-filled, loving world. The Seraphim know every truth of who you are as a soul. They know everything that brings you joy. They want to see your life filled with all that brings you joy so you can live in joy and Oneness more, and more, and more!

The Seraphim are helping you work through challenges, take action to serve humanity, and live your joy.

It's time for you to spend time with Saraphina and the Seraphim angels. Get into Oneness and ask them:

1. Saraphina, are you working with me? If so, how?

2. Please show me my soul's role in creating a new Earth.

3. What step would you have me take first?

4. How can I serve/take action and better care for myself at the same time?

5. What sign, number, or color do you use to communicate your presence in my life?

6. Is there anything else you want me to know?

ARCHANGEL GABRIELLE

Like our souls, angels are genderless. Archangel Gabrielle is seen by some as male (aka Archangel Gabriel) and others as female. When I connect with Archangel Gabrielle on this, they say the more accurate term is non-binary, so throughout this chapter you'll see me use they/them pronouns (the same pronouns I use for God as well). Archangel Gabrielle is an advocate for you living your life as your true, authentic self, and they're here to help you know yourself in order to express yourself fully.

Archangel Gabrielle is one of the most well-known angels and is famous for helping with communication. Archangel Gabrielle is here to help you:

1. Learn to communicate with loved ones on the Other Side and your angels.

2. Hear your intuition more clearly.

3. Understand yourself better so that you can speak your needs from your throat chakra more clearly.

4. Communicate with living family members. Especially in difficult conversations with your spouse, child, parents, and close friends.

5. Speak with confidence on stage, in small groups, or when working with others.

6. Speak up or ask for a raise at work.

7. Use your voice to assist divine feminine rising and advocate for the equality of all souls on Earth.

8. Anytime you are called to speak in any way, you can be sure Archangel Gabrielle is right by your side.

Have you ever cried and heard someone say, "Don't stop your tears, just let them fall. It's energy within you that needs to be released?" This concept applies to the energy within you that needs to be spoken. Most people do not speak enough. Instead, they hold their thoughts, feelings, and emotions inside. Over time, this energy builds up within and needs to be released. Why do people hold things within instead of speaking? Because it's what they were taught to do.

When you were young, did your parents ever say:

- ⌘ "Eat all of your dinner or you're not getting dessert."
- ⌘ "Suck it up."
- ⌘ "Boys don't cry."
- ⌘ "Who do you think you are?"
- ⌘ "Put a sock in it."
- ⌘ "Don't make waves."

Like our school system, all of these sayings were part of a culture used to create robotic human workers unable to listen to their intuition, taught not to be empathic, but to simply "fall in line."

Our parents said these things to us because their parents said similar things to them, and the generation before them and so on.

We were taught to hide our soul-self. We were taught to be "good" and not "stir up any trouble" by speaking or being ourselves. We were taught to ignore our inner voice. As children, many of us carried this over into adulthood. Over time, we were socialized to hold our thoughts, feelings, emotions within ourselves and not speak.

Although, anyone with this habit knows that it creates a volcanic energy internally that will explode outwardly, in one way or another. Not being yourself and not speaking up, creates pent-up tension within. Because you've been trained to not speak, not to be yourself, and not to listen to the voice within, you look to society to tell you who to be. You allow society to show you an alternative way to release this pent-up energy, which is where addictions, vices, and trying to be something you're not all come into play.

This system creates work-a-holics, shop-a-holics, alcohol or drug addictions, relationship problems, workout-a-holics, eating disorders, drama-a-holics, gamblers, etc.

We search for something to buy, someone to marry, a job title or salary that will fix it all, but nothing outside of us can permanently fix what's deeply broken, which is the fact that you are a soul here to live out your purpose and your joy, and you were taught not to. Friend, the reality is, only you can heal this wound by getting to know yourself and what brings you joy; loving yourself, and allowing yourself to be who you truly are by radiating love to this world by fully expressing, speaking and living your truth.

How do we do this? We stop allowing society to dictate what success means to us or what our lives should look like. We stop living to please other people and start living to please ourselves. Friend, while your soul can never be damaged, allowing society or the people within your life to fully dictate your life can damage your spirit.

Your spirit is your inner cheerleader, excited, and passionate about life! Archangel Gabrielle says that when we do not speak our truth with love, we hide away our inner cheerleader and with it goes our passion and excitement for life. We become resentful and a shadow of our former selves. However, the more we speak what is in our hearts, the more we stand in our true authentic energy and radiate love out to the world.

Learning to speak with love will change this planet. Archangel Gabrielle says none of us have learned this lesson entirely, we are all still working on it (on the podcast I say, "We all must do the work," and this is what I mean)!

Archangel Gabrielle asks you to look at this from a different perspective. Not speaking and taking action on the callings within your heart (both big and small), robs you of your joy. I work with people every day who do not know who they are. How can a person speak their truth if they do not know who they are? Friend, I cannot tell you the number of 40, 50, 60, and 70 year olds that I've worked with regularly to help them remember who they are as a soul, what brings them joy in this lifetime, and how to shed the layers of the past to finally live their joy.

Archangel Gabrielle needs you to hear that it's never too late to do your work and begin living a life you love!

Friend, this life was intended to be joy-filled. We're all surely going to have our share of challenges, but we've got that part down. What we haven't nailed down is living this life with more joy! If you are an empath wanting to return to your own energy, your joy is the place to start!

Archangel Gabrielle teaches that the way to come back to yourself is through what brings you joy. What brings you joy is different from what brings me joy because your joy is one of the most true reflections of your soul's energy in this life. If you could bottle the energy of your joy, it would be like bottling the energy of your soul. Your joy is you, and it's the way to begin feeling your own energy again after this world has tried to fit you in a box of its own making! Thankfully, you never fit into that box and you never will. The way back to yourself is through what brings you joy.

How do you get back to your joy? Archangel Gabrielle always gives my clients the same tool. They say, "I want you to create a 'Joy List', a list of all the things that bring you joy. You cannot create this list overnight. Continue to add to this list for one whole year. Each time you find that something brings you joy (big or small), write it down on your list." This could be a favorite song, food, movie, activity, person, place, or thing. Archangel Gabrielle says by the end of one year, you'll have a list of all the things that bring you joy.

After one year, separate these items out into what you can realistically do each day, week, month, and year to feed yourself more joy. Select items from each category and give yourself more joy. When you feed yourself joy, you live in your own energy more. As you become reacquainted with your energy, you know what you want more and more, and you begin taking responsibility for your life. Knowing what you want allows you to speak from that confident space and in doing so, you co-create (with God) the beautiful life you were meant to live.

You have two assignments with Archangel Gabrielle. First, get into Oneness and connect with them so that you can get to know them better. Ask them the questions below. The second exercise is to work on your joy list. Write down every big and little thing that brings you joy. Return to this list and add to it over the course of a year. After one year, seperate your joys out into what you can do each day, week, month and year.

1. Archangel Gabrielle, what did I experience in my life that stopped me from being me and speaking my truth?

2. What is the best path for me to get back to myself?

3. Are there others in my life who I can share my joy and radiate love into the world with? What are their names?

4. Archangel Gabrielle, what signs, colors or numbers do you use to communicate with me in my life? How will I know when you are around?

_____

_____

_____

_____

_____

MY JOY LIST

For one year, create a list of everything, big and small, that brings you joy.

MY JOYS

Categorize your joys based on what you can do each day, week, month and year.
Then feed yourself more of your joys!

Day	Week	Month	Year

ANGEL COMMUNICATION

Part 1: Week Three

If you're in the Angel Membership,
go to the Angel Communication Part 1 course
(in the folder titled *A Year With Your Angels*):

☐ Watch the following videos:
- ☐ **Archangel Raphael**
- ☐ **Archangel Ariel**
- ☐ **Archangel Sandalphon and the Cherubs**
- ☐ **Archangel Raguel**

ARCHANGEL RAPHAEL

Every hair on your head, every cell within your body and every muscle, ligament, and organ within you is known by Archangel Raphael. He is constantly working with you to keep your body at optimum health. Archangel Raphael doesn't work alone. He reminds me of the 1990's rapper DMX and The Ruff Ryders. I just loved how any time DMX came onto the MTV Music Award stage to accept an award, he'd bring his whole crew of 30+ people up with him. Archangel Raphael is the same way in that when you see him, he's always surrounded by angels, standing behind him and at his sides.

Archangel Raphael has enough angels working for him to provide each person on Earth with an entire angel team to energetically manage their physical health. When I work with a client who is sick, suffering from cancer or another illness, Archangel Raphael always steps in to show that he has already given this person a team of "doctor angels." These angels assist you, your actual doctors, nurses, and health care professionals in your journey to complete physical health.

When you hear a voice within (your inner dialogue) asking you to go to the doctor and get something checked out or to take better care of your physical health in some way, it is the voice of Archangel Raphael speaking to you. Archangel Raphael works with your doctors, nurses, and therapists to encourage you to seek the help you need from a medical professional first and foremost.

As I write this, he's reminding me of a soul I've worked with in many sessions. This man had a successful career as a chiropractor, when he became sick with cancer. He refused to work with medical doctors because he wanted to heal his cancer holistically, but he passed away. Friend, this soul spoke loud and clear like he was shouting from Heaven. His message was, "I did not need to die. I wish I would've worked with medical professionals so that I did not leave my beautiful young family behind."

Friend, do not attempt to heal yourself with *only* holistic remedies or prayer. Utilize the doctors and medical advancements God gave us together with prayer, holistic, energy healing, and spiritual therapies that you first clear with your professional medical team.

Archangel Raphael also works with us in a way that relates to how people in our families have passed away. He shows me that humans worry about passing in the same way our parents and grandparents passed. When a manner of death like a heart disease, cancer, or Alzheimer's runs in the family, Archangel Raphael says people fear they will also get it because it "runs in the family." This can breed an almost obsessive fear within our thoughts. Archangel Raphael says it is possible to worry so much that we do in fact manifest those ailments in our lives when those ailments were never supposed to impact us in the first place. He works to stop us from doing this to ourselves. Archangel Raphael says that we must stay on top of our health by visiting the right doctors and doing what work we can to prevent these ailments. Additionally, we must be working to change our thoughts by rewriting the stories within our minds and seeing ourselves as fully healthy.

Often in a session, Archangel Raphael will ask a client to picture themselves as a 90, 100+ year old person who is fully healthy both mentally and physically. He'll ask them to see themselves at a birthday or anniversary celebration with their partner, children, grandchildren, family, and friends surrounding them. He asks the person to feel immense gratitude in that future moment. Daydreaming about the future you want and feeling good emotions associated with that future event are the two biggest keys to manifestation and co-creation work. It is the feeling and emotion that builds an invisible bridge and takes you where you want to go.

Through my work with Archangel Raphael, I've also learned every experience you have, whether it's looking at your phone, reading an email, having a conversation—every single experience you have is energy that is being filtered through you in a specific process that impacts your physical health.

It all starts with your three fields of energy: the energy of your auric field, your chakras, and your physical body.

You filter your energy through your experiences, first felt in the outer layer of your auric field about five feet in front of you. When you sweep a feeling or emotion "under the rug" instead of honoring it, looking at it, and dealing with it, you're actually magnifying that energy and drawing it closer to your chakras. As you continue to ignore your emotions, you draw this energy into your chakras. If you do not deal directly with your feelings and emotions while they're in your chakras, this energy moves into your physical body and begins to compound.

Once inside the physical body, this stagnant energy is like fruit sitting on a countertop. If you let fruit sit for too long it rots. Subconsciously, you think that because you're not dealing with this energy it's going to magically go away on its own, but the opposite is true. Stagnant energy within you festers and creates dis-ease.

Creating a life of ease requires conscious effort to process your feelings and emotions, and take actions to support yourself. Without conscious effort, we automatically fall into the chaotic lifestyle that society has forced on us. Society has created a blueprint for a life of constant activity where we're checking our phones 24/7, 365; being bombarded by noise everywhere we go; pushing ourselves past our limit, in the name of "productivity"; and constantly judging/critiquing ourselves and everyone we meet. When we participate in a productivity-centered life, there is no time or space for us, nor is there time or space for us to process our feelings or emotions.

Society's blueprint for our lives leads to a life of dis-ease.

Life does not have to be this way, friend. We can choose to turn the phones off and unplug. We can choose to make silence, stillness, and Oneness a priority in our lives. We can do our work to rewire our minds and work through our need to be perfect robots who are constantly producing, and whose only value is in how much they can produce. We can choose to make our mental and physical health a priority, and find joy in people and experiences rather than things.

When we take responsibility for our complete health, we keep our energy clear. We feel more of our soul's energy instead of the anxieties and fears of this world, and we can literally feel our physical bodies vibrating at a higher frequency because we feel good!

Archangel Raphael is part of your Spirit Team, and works with you to keep your energy clear and your body healthy. He uses different methods to help you in this process:

1. Changing the stories within your mind so the emotions within your body change as well

2. Working through and releasing past pain buried energetically within the body

3. Taking action through movement and food that help your body vibrate at the highest frequency possible

4. For those who are sick with illness or disease, Archangel Raphael encourages you to work with the right doctors and healthcare professionals, and he magnifies their healing efforts whenever possible

If you're looking to make changes in your life, don't be overwhelmed. Archangel Raphael works to create long-lasting change within your life, one step at a time. Start here: Archangel Raphael says your double helix DNA strand is made up of billions of doors and windows where you have freewill to close those that limit your health and open those that access your most healthy self. He often asks my clients to say this prayer:

Dear God,

Please close all the doors and windows to my DNA that are not serving my highest health and open all the doors and windows to my DNA that would serve my highest health! Thank you God!

Amen

It's time for you to connect with Archangel Raphael. Get into Oneness and ask Archangel Raphael to spend some time with you. Ask him the questions below.

NOTE: Archangel Raphael will always ask you to work with at least one medical doctor. The responses you get are great topics to address with your therapist and medical professionals.

1. What am I most concerned about, consciously and subconsciously regarding my own health? What fears about my own health do I need to work through?

2. Are there medical professionals I should be working with that I am not already?

3. Archangel Raphael, what vision of my future should I hold to combat my fear based thoughts?

4. How would you have me create a life of better health, more flow, and more ease?

5. Archangel Raphael, what signs, colors or numbers do you use to communicate with me in my life? How will I know when you are around?

_____

_____

_____

_____

_____

_____

ARCHANGEL ARIEL

When I was going through the previously mentioned turbulent time in my life, and everything felt like it was falling apart, I had a strong feeling I needed to get a dog. I wanted a puppy who would help me feel love again, who wouldn't look at me like I was constantly messing things up. I needed unconditional love in my life and I knew owning a dog would bring the love I so desperately needed to feel again. After bringing our Shih Tzu "Fluff" home, all energies around me started to shift. My energy, my husband's energy, the energy in our home, the vibration of everything around me was elevated. I immediately knew Fluff was both clearing energy and holding the vibration of Oneness within our home.

It's important to note this strong feeling to get a dog came months after my dad passed and it wasn't the first time I had a calling within my heart to own a dog. In college, my dad had asked me what I wanted for graduation. We hadn't spoken in years, but had recently reconnected at the time. My dad suggested we go on a European trip together to visit my uncle who lived abroad, but all I really wanted was a dog, so I asked for a puppy. I don't remember what happened, but something occurred between then and graduation and we stopped talking again. I never got the puppy or the trip with my dad, and it upset me. Fast forward to being an adult and feeling called to be a pet owner, I could feel my dad's presence with me every time I thought about getting a dog. It was like my dad was trying to make up for not getting me a dog for graduation. He was working on the Other Side to ensure I had a dog in my life now, but the synchronicities didn't stop there.

My dad was using the dog to communicate another message. He was trying to show me that a sign I had seen before (and had second guessed) was indeed real. The morning of my dad's memorial service, my sister and I stopped at the grocery store to be helpful and pick up some items his family needed. We stopped dead in our tracks when we saw a full display, floor to ceiling, of Fluffernutter, the gooey marshmallow spread that comes in a jar. Fluffernutter sandwiches were my dad's jam! Only he didn't call the stuff "Fluffernutter," he called it "Fluff." It was his special thing and until that day I'd never seen a display of the stuff in a grocery store. When we saw the display on the day of my dad's memorial I knew it was a sign from him. He was with us.

How is Fluffernutter connected to me getting a dog? That's the second message in this angel story. I didn't pick my dog's name. My husband and daughter did. I first convinced my husband to get a dog by telling him, "I'm getting a dog and if you don't like it, you know where the door is." It was not a healthy way to communicate, but that's where we were in our marriage back then, and I was just learning to use my voice. My husband got onboard and talked about the dog's name for weeks at the dinner table. We took a paper plate and wrote name possibilities all over it. My husband and daughter settled on the name Fluff. It didn't dawn on me until months later!

One day my dad brought it to my attention during an Automatic Writing session. I saw in my imagination the memory of my sister and I in front of the large display of Fluffernutter. Once I recalled that memory, my dad flipped to another memory within my mind of the time in college when he promised to get me a dog. Spirit uses our imagination to communicate messages, which is why you must not second guess something you don't understand, when it comes to mind. Know it is them trying to communicate with you in a different way.

My dad was communicating messages through an animal: 1) This dog was from him. 2) He was present with my family from the Other Side. 3) He was not only communicating to me through my inner dialogue. My dad was speaking to my daughter and husband, communicating the name Fluff to them through their inner dialogues as well. These messages gave me peace, despite the fact that I felt like everything was falling apart at the time. My dad was assisting from the Other Side, and it made me feel like somehow, someway everything was going to be alright.

I tell this story to help you understand Archangel Ariel's energy better. Animals absolutely shift energies within ourselves, our families, our homes, our lives, and on the planet in general. Archangel Ariel works together with souls on your Spirit Team to help bring pets to you when they're needed.

I've learned so much from Archangel Ariel about animals over the years. She says our pets are tuning forks. They automatically hold the high vibration of Oneness. Dogs also have a natural filtration system. They hold Oneness and filter all other vibrations around them through Oneness, helping raise the vibration of their environment. Some owners fear that the animal takes on the negativity themselves into their own body, but Archangel Ariel says that is rarely the case. We can learn to do energy work on our animals and they absolutely love it! Not because they need their energy cleared, but because they love living in Oneness and they feel energy palpably when you send them God's vibration.

When the sad day comes for our pets to cross over to the Other Side, Archangel Ariel is there to help them and us. She's shown me that only animals who do not have owners on Earth go to an animal Heaven. Animals that do have owners almost always go to their owners' home on the Other Side to wait for them there. Animals are part of our soul family. Any deeply special pet from this life is part of your Spirit Team when they cross over. Sometimes a pet that comes to us in this life was actually a child or family member in a past life.

I was at a friend's house when I understood this on a deeper level. My friend owns three horses and has no biological children of her own. I went out to meet the horses for the first time and heard them audibly in my inner dialogue. "We are her children," they said. I stopped walking as they showed me a vision of three human children running and playing by my friend's side in a past life. The horses said souls can come through as animals to comfort the ones they love. They showed me my symbol for the Spirit Team, a circle, and put themselves inside the circle. The horses signaled they too were part of my friend's team, even though they were still alive here on Earth. They said that because all souls have a Higher Self, any living soul's Higher Self can be on a person's Spirit Team.

In a session, some animals show me that after their passing, they will reincarnate and come back to their owner in the body of a new pet. They say their owner does not want to be without them in this lifetime, so they will continue finding their way back to their owner for the duration of that person's life. Other animals show me themselves with their owner only for an animal-lifetime or two, but they will say their spirit stays with you.

For example, when I'm in a session, I sometimes see the spirit of a dog or cat right next to the legs of my client the entire appointment. Spirit doesn't normally do this. They will step forward, say something, and then step back. These animals show their presence the entire time and Archangel Ariel says the spirit of these loyal animals never leaves their owners' side. Instead, some deceased pets hold Oneness and filter their owner's energy even from the Other Side.

You can ask Archangel Ariel to help you connect with your pets in Heaven through Automatic Writing as well. You can talk to them, just as you're learning to talk to your angels. When you try this, connect with only one pet at a time. Otherwise the energy can become overwhelming and be difficult for you to sort out who is talking.

Archangel Ariel is also the angel presiding over nature and the plant kingdom. I have more work to do with her in this arena, but I want to share a story with you. Currently, Archangel Ariel has me doing an experiment, raising the vibration of my body through food. She's had me eating more raw fruits and veggies than ever before. When I do, my body feels physically different. She says that colors play a role as well. Have you ever heard someone say, "Eat the rainbow?" Archangel Ariel says that there is a different vibrational frequency for each color and that all color vibrations are vital to our energy. She also says that plants, fruits and veggies derive and hold the most Oneness energy, which is transferred into our bodies when we eat them.

I find that as I try this, I'm not eating to feel full, but to feel my body vibrating at an even higher frequency to feel more Oneness. Again, I have much work to do in this area, but you can experiment with this concept as well by connecting with Archangel Ariel in Automatic Writing, eating more fruits and veggies, and noting the vibration of your body after each meal. Allow Archangel Ariel to guide you and teach you more!

In addition to working with nature and animals, Archangel Ariel also assists the Seraphim with the rise of the divine feminine. It's important to note some things: 1) The divine feminine is rising to be at an equal level with divine masculine. 2) The energies of the divine feminine are not that of the prim, proper "good girl" who is alway sunshine and rainbows. Nature energy and animal energy are divine feminine energies. Mother nature is a divine feminine energy, constantly birthing new creations and life into this world. Her strength is the most powerful force on this planet. Archangel Ariel says the divine feminine are energies in motion, through action.

We must activate the divine feminine energy within us by taking action ourselves.

Friend, the world is not going to save itself, and the angels and God will not bypass our freewill. If you do not want to take action, Spirit cannot force you. It is up to us to make the decision for ourselves. Spirit says the issues of the work at hand are now too large for one person to tackle alone. Each person must do their part. We can no longer look around and say, "Other people are taking action so I don't need to." No—every single soul here on Earth is being called to rise with love. Your angels are calling you to be Oneness energy in motion, through loving action—to save the planet and solve the problems of the world. Archangel Ariel says there has never been a time with more potential to make true lasting changes than there is right now. In order to do this, each of us is being called to take action and mute the voice of doubt within our own Egoic Minds.

In order for true, lasting solutions to change our world and our lives, Archangel Ariel says we must:

1. Learn and research

2. Listen, believe, and be led by those most deeply impacted

3. Work to lessen our Egoic Minds and continually humble ourselves

4. Take stead-fast, loving action to fulfill the desires of those most deeply impacted

5. Rest, recharge, live in joy

6. Dedicate ourselves to a lifetime of learning and unlearning so we never have to return to the current state of the world

Taking action isn't about you at all. It is about you stepping out of your Egoic Mind, putting the collective human race in front of your own desires, and lovingly serving all (even those you don't agree with). Taking action is being the physical incarnation of Oneness in motion.

When each person takes action (in the way their heart is called), the puzzle pieces will fall into place and the vibration of this planet will rise.

It's time for you to connect with Archangel Ariel. Get into Oneness and ask Archangel Ariel to spend time with you. Here are some topics to talk to her about through Automatic Writing. Write down any information she brings to you.

1. Ask Archangel Ariel any questions that arise within you about your pets (past, present or future).

2. How can connecting with nature or plants benefit my life more? How would you have me work with nature and plant energy?

3. Ask Archangel Ariel to show you what your role is in divine feminine rising. How can my soul best serve humanity? What is the long-term goal I can help achieve? What action would you have me take first?

4. Archangel Ariel, what signs, colors or numbers do you use to communicate with me in my life? How will I know when you are around?

_____

_____

_____

_____

_____

_____

_____

_____

_____

_____

ARCHANGEL SANDALPHON AND THE CHERUBIM ANGELS

To understand Archangel Sandalphon, you must understand the Cherubim Angels (aka Cherub), the angels depicted as children in paintings. It's true that these angels are small, but they're even smaller than you may think. Cherubs are the vessel of Oneness that holds the vibration of Oneness itself.

Remember learning that you have over 37.2 trillion cells within your body and that Spirit says you have more than 37.2 trillion angels working with you? Here's how this works: everything is energy which vibrates at different frequencies. The smallest piece of all matter is God-energy. Scientists say that the atom is 99.9% space—that 99.9% is God-energy and the energy of your soul.

Here on Earth, we humans have a kind of amnesia about who we truly are, and we are socialized to feel the vibrations of this Earth (fear, anxiety, stress, sadness, etc). Awakening is a remembrance of who we are as souls on the Other Side (we are love, joy, peace, bliss, ease, grace) and beginning to live from our soul-selves here.

God didn't send you here to live a miserable life of pain and suffering.

Every moment of your life you've had direct access to God's energy and you always will. Angels are extensions of God's energy. Some religions say Cherubs are the closest to God's energy because they hold the space for God's energy and we can never be disconnected from it. This is what I see as well. It is the Cherubs job to be Oneness and hold the portal door open for you to get into Oneness at any time; they do this by accessing the 99.9% space in your body's 37.2 trillion cells and the over 37.2 trillion invisible atoms in your auric field—Cherubs occupy all of the space within you and surrounding you.

The Cherubs' job is to be and hold the door to Oneness open for you so you can step into God-vibration at any time, whereas Archangel Sandalphon's job is to guide you to and through the door! Archangel Sandalphon's responsibility is to help you return to Oneness by awakening. As we talked about in the chapter on Oneness, you cannot rush yourself to awaken because it can overload your psyche. Archangel Sandalphon helps you to unfold at the pace that is right for you, regardless of how frustrating it may be to your Egoic Mind (which wants to awaken more quickly).

Archangel Sandalphon guides you to awaken in many ways, and one of the most significant is through signs. More and more people around the world are waking up to see angel numbers. Why? Because every time you see a number sign, your mind awakens out of sleep and becomes conscious that you are not your thoughts, but the *observer* of your thoughts!

When you see angel numbers 10, 20, 30+ times a day you're breaking the cycle of unconsciousness and building brain-memory of how to hold Oneness, how to stay in the present moment. Every time you receive a gift of signs from your Angels, pause and thank them for the work they're doing with you. Then ask yourself, "What was I just thinking about?" Know that your Spirit Team is trying to communicate that they are helping you with that too!

Archangel Sandalphon not only helps you receive angel signs, but also connects you with signs from your loved ones in Heaven, as well as to clearly hear the answers to your prayers. When you feel you're not getting messages or feel unsure that what you're hearing is from your angels, ask Angel Sandalphon for help!

You can say this:

> *Dear Archangel Sandalphon,*
>
> *Please help me clearly identify signs from my angels, guides, and loved ones in Heaven. Please help me clearly receive, hear, and understand the messages they have for me so that I know it's them guiding me!*
>
> *Amen*

Try connecting with Archangel Sandalphon now, asking him the following questions and writing down what comes to you! Remember to get into a state of Oneness first.

1. What signs do my angels send me to help my consciousness awaken?

2. What signs do my loved ones in Heaven send me?

3. How can I be sure that I've heard an answer to my prayers?

4. Archangel Sandalphon, what signs, colors or numbers do you use to communicate with me in my life? How will I know when you are around?

ARCHANGEL RAGUEL

The essence of God and your soul is love, joy, peace, bliss, ease, and grace, but being in this world means we feel other lower vibrations like anxiety, fear, stress, frustration, sadness, fury, or rage (because they are currently part of the collective consciousness). I've heard it said before that it is not known where thought and consciousness come from. Humans do not think about what they should think about, thoughts just come in.

In a similar fashion, most times we do not want to feel negative emotions running through us but they too just come in. Take the emotion of rage for example. When you are triggered the negative energy is just there with you in a flash. When we feel lower emotions or triggers they are an indicator that we have work to do within. We must look at these lower vibrations within us and understand them in order to release them from our energy field. When we do this work we retain our power and our state of Oneness; however, when we believe the lower emotion we give our power to it, allow it to control us and in doing so lose our connection to Oneness.

Archangel Raguel is best suited to help us with this work. He says the first step is being honest with yourself. Many of us do not want to be honest with ourselves because it is scary. When we're honest with ourselves we may find that we want to change jobs, work more deeply on a challenge with a spouse, rebuild a broken relationship or a part of ourselves that is wounded and tender.

When Archangel Raguel steps in, he doesn't hold the energy of your trigger, he holds the energy of your wound.

I worked with a client who had recently been diagnosed with cancer and wanted to work through rage within her heart, which she had suppressed for decades. We worked with Archangel Raguel as she was on my massage table, and he helped me guide her through a visual meditation with her Inner Child to find the source of her anger. As we went back in time with her angels, a forgotten memory resurfaced for her. She said when she was young, school children did not eat together in the cafeteria. Instead, they were sent home to eat lunch. In this memory, she saw herself hungry every day because her mom never fed her lunch and as a small child she did not know how to make anything for herself. She recalled being so excited every time her classmate would invite her over for lunch because that classmate's mother would make them lunch and she would feel full.

As I continued the Angel Reiki session, I could feel within her how this past experience was the equivalent of a gigantic open wound within her energy field. Being honest with herself was not easy because it meant feeling painful emotions she had repressed for decades; Archangel Raguel helped us to heal this energetically.

He showed the woman herself as a child feeling alone, hungry, unloved, and unwanted by her mother. He showed her the pain her mother had experienced, not to bypass her hurt, but to help her understand that her mother's neglect stemmed from deep past pain she had not worked through, herself. Archangel Raguel often helps us realize the truth of the sayings, "Hurt people, hurt people," and "Pain not transformed is transmitted." He went on to show her how proud of her, her Spirit Team was for breaking the lineage and not carrying this pain into her relationship with her own children as an adult. They showed her how she could've neglected her own children as her mother had done to her, but she chose to shower them with the love that she craved as a child.

At one point in the session, Archangel Raguel showed the client her mother's life review in Heaven and how she had to step into the body and mind of her daughter to experience all of the ways she had harmed her daughter for herself. From Heaven, this mother looked at her adult child with tears streaming down her face and showed true remorse for all the hurt she had caused. The mother showed her daughter how her neglect triggered a series of events in her daughter's life, all stemming from the lack of worthiness she felt within herself as a child. The mother and daughter grieved the pain she caused, together and she expressed to her daughter how much she truly loved and adored her, and how proud she was of her from the Other Side.

All of life's challenges are delicate and require discernment.

The mother's remorse does not and cannot make up for the neglectful harm she caused in this lifetime, but for my client it did bring a sense of peace to hear her mother say, "I'll forever be sorry for what I did. I ask for your forgiveness. I love you and think you to be the most beautiful human being. I'm proud of the mother you are to your children and I will make this up to you."

Call on Archangel Raguel when you are triggered in your life, and he will help you to see the situation from each person's perspective and create boundaries in your life that protect your heart. Know that when you feel triggered, Archangel Raguel does not hold that emotion. Instead, he is able to see the big picture. He can see how every soul has been emotionally damaged, and holds the vibration of peace-filled resolution as he helps you heal your deepest wounds.

Archangel Raguel is the angel to call on if you ever find yourself in a legal situation or legal mediation. Call on him to help you find the solution God desires for all parties. Ask Archangel Raguel to help you hear your intuition clearly on all legal matters so that you know which way to go at all times. Hire the best lawyer you can afford and have faith within your heart, knowing that God is leading the way.

Friend, some people have survived major physical and emotional attacks. If this is you, Archangel Raguel does not ask you to relive these, to see the other person's perspective, or invite them back into your life. Archangel Raguel and I ask you not to do this work alone. Please only do this work with a professional, licensed therapist. You can call on Archangel Raguel to be there and he will be. He will bring you peace and comfort as you work with a therapist on your past.

If you do not have major trauma in your past, you may choose to flex your discernment and work with Archangel Raguel, but if at any time this work becomes too heavy you must bring it to your therapist and work directly with them from there on out.

When connecting with Archangel Raguel, here are some questions you can ask:

1. What are my current triggers?

2. Which past emotional wounds magnify my triggers even more? Then work with a therapist to work through past emotional wounds, set boundaries, see the story from other perspectives and find more peace within your heart.

3. Archangel Raguel, what signs, colors or numbers do you use to communicate with me in my life? How will I know when you are around?

_____

_____

_____

_____

_____

_____

_____

ANGEL COMMUNICATION

Part 1: Week Four

If you're in the Angel Membership,
go to the Angel Communication Part 1 course
(in the folder titled *A Year With Your Angels*):

☐ Watch the following videos:
    ☐ **Archangel Raziel**
    ☐ **Archangel Haniel**
    ☐ **Archangel Chamuel**
    ☐ **Archangel Azrael**
    ☐ **Archangel Jeremiel**

ARCHANGEL RAZIEL

Every moment of your life, you are working on one of three puzzles:

1. The life lesson right in front of you is your current puzzle
2. Your overall life plan is a bigger puzzle made up of all your smaller life lesson puzzles
3. Finally, your big life plan puzzle also fits into an even greater puzzle made up of all the lives you've ever lived

When I see a puzzle within my imagination during a session, I know Archangel Raziel is there to talk about what my client is currently working through in their life. When he takes that small lesson puzzle and plugs it into your overall life puzzle, I know this means that what you are going through is significant to your life's purpose. At times, he will take it one step further than that and will take your overall life puzzle, and connect it to your past lives. When I see this, I know it means that what you're working through has carried over from a past life and we need to talk about that. Your past lives, your current life, and your current life lesson all fit together in an intricate way. Archangel Raziel knows every detail of it all.

Archangel Raziel knows your life plan, your life's purpose, your God-given gifts and how all of this ties together and unfolds in your everyday life. When possible, he encourages you to enjoy the mysteries of life as it all unfolds in front of you, but he knows that this life is not easy. Archangel Raziel reveres you for the strength and courage it takes to be here during life's most challenging moments, and he is here to help you make sense of it all.

Have you ever heard of the Akashic Records? The Akashic Records is a place where you can look at the history of your soul. Every moment of your soul's existence is recorded in the Akashic Records. You can go learn about every past life you've ever lived, why you are here now in this one, what your purpose is and what action would best serve you right now in your life. Here's the caveat, the Akashic Records can be "Pandora's Box." When you open "Pandora's Box" there is so much inside that it is difficult to close. The same goes for the Akashic Records, for some people. Some misuse the Akashic Records and fall off their path in this lifetime.

Some people want to know every detail about every past life they've ever lived. They will travel to the Akashic Records as they sleep and waste years researching files that do not have any link to this lifetime they're in right now. What do I mean? Archangel Raziel says that if you've lived 1,000 lifetimes, you've healed and worked through 99.9% of your past life lessons. In those past 1,000 lifetimes you went through some pretty major tragedies, but you also healed from them. They're over and done, and your soul has moved on.

At times, when people go to the Akashic Records to look at "everything" they see tragedies they've healed from, but their current mind doesn't remember that healing and becomes fixated on what they went through before. When you do this to yourself, you're actually taking yourself off your life path in this lifetime. You are wasting your precious life here and using the Akashic Records in a way it was not intended to be used.

The best way to use the Akashic Records is to pray:

> *Dear God,*
>
> *As I sleep tonight, please allow my soul to travel to the Akashic Records to better understand only what I'm working through right now in my life, and how it fits into my life's purpose. If what I'm working through ties into a past life lesson I did not fully work through, please show me that as well. God, while my soul travels to the Akashic Records, please allow my body to be fully rested and recharged so that I can live my best day yet tomorrow.*
>
> *Amen*

As you sleep, Archangel Raziel will take your consciousness to the Akashic Records for your soul to get the answers to current life questions you've been searching for. Some people do this when they are awake during Automatic Writing (both work well). Archangel Raziel says that when your soul goes to the Akashic Records, it's visiting a place where there is no time. As your body sleeps for eight+ hours, your soul may take a month of time researching over there, but your life here will not change. Most people do not remember being at the Akashic Records or the amount of time they spent there.

After visiting the Akashic Records, you will see the answers you've been searching for appear like magic in your life. You must have faith, believe, keep your heart open and the answers will appear before you. You will know with certainty the direction you want to go in your life. You'll know the next action step to take. By doing this work with Archangel Raziel and traveling to the Akashic Records, you'll see the puzzle pieces you've been searching for fall into place in divine time.

Archangel Raziel helps you to clear blocks of negative or distorted thinking so that you can co-create the life your soul was born to live with God. When you are confident of your path, you do not allow negative thoughts to stop or block you. You become an expert manifestor/co-creator in your life!

Archangel Raziel works with every soul on Earth, though those who are goal driven may find themselves working with him more because they are the quickest manifestors. Driven people struggle more with truly enjoying life because they love spending all their time working with Archangel Raziel to see just how far they can go in this lifetime (I know because I'm one of those people). It's a fun game to them.

Your God-given gifts are part of your life path and your life plan. I've witnessed many people want and ask God for a specific gift, but what they do not understand is how powerful the gifts they were given truly are. Archangel Raziel wants you to picture this image within your imagination: first, see every soul as omnipresent. Like God, your soul can be in multiple places at once. The "Higher Self" of each person is on the Other Side. Each Higher Self knows which souls on Earth they must rely on in this lifetime for support to get where they are going. Your soul's purpose ties into the paths of other souls whether it be family, friends, or strangers. Archangel Raziel asks you to see that behind your back are perhaps millions of souls (the Higher Self of millions of souls) pushing you forward because they know that when you do take action toward your purpose, you will positively influence their paths here on Earth—and they, too, will be able to succeed in their life's purpose.

Archangel Raziel needed you to see this so that you understand your gifts are not supposed to look like someone else's you've seen on TV. If you wish for their gifts instead of your own, you will not be able to support all the souls you are here to impact. You were born to be uniquely yourself and the more you allow yourself to be fully and authentically you, the more you fulfill your purpose in this lifetime. All you have to do (at any time) is follow the vibration of Oneness, your intuition, and your soul's voice.

I asked Archangel Raziel if there's any additional information that he'd like you to know. He said that his sign to you is a rainbow. I admit, I questioned this at first but then he said, "Go to your Angels and Awakening Podcast Tribe group on Facebook." I did as instructed, and there was a post waiting to be approved that spoke of rainbows and showed a magnificent rainbow in the sky. Okay Archangel Raziel, I get it—message received! When you feel down about your path, need validation you're on the right track or want to know you're really working with Archangel Raziel look for the rainbow sign.

It's time for you to connect with Archangel Raziel. Get into Oneness and ask Archangel Raziel questions about what you're currently working on in your life.

1. You can ask your own questions or, "What life lesson am I currently working on right now in my life? How does this lesson tie into my life plan? What action step would you have me take next or over the course of this year?"

2. Also ask Archangel Raziel, "What are my God-given gifts and how am I to be using them?"

3. Before you go to sleep, ask Archangel Raziel to take you to the Akashic Records and say the prayer, "God, as I sleep tonight, please allow my soul to travel to the Akashic Records to understand what I'm working through right now in my life, how it fits into my life's purpose. If what I'm working through ties into a past life lesson I did not fully work through, please show me that as well. God, while my soul travels to the Akashic Records, please allow my body to be fully rested and recharged so that I can live my best day yet tomorrow. Amen."

In the days/weeks following, record the answers that come to you, and ask Archangel Raziel to provide validation by showing you a rainbow!

_____

_____

_____

_____

_____

_____

_____

_____

_____

_____

_____

ARCHANGEL HANIEL

In order to understand Archangel Haniel, we must look at what it means to be a healer. When you hear the word "healer" you might think of a reiki practitioner, angel messenger, chiropractor, naturopath, intuitive, psychic medium or other related healing art. However, through Archangel Haniel I've learned that healers are souls who feel called to serve God over everything else. Healers pray, "God, please use my life and allow me to be a tool you can work through to serve humanity. My life is yours, God. Lead me." Healers are people here to serve humanity in every line of work.

I've worked with clients Archangel Haniel calls "lawyer healers," "CEO healers," "marketing healers," "doctor healers," "accountant healers," and so on. Name your type of work and there are healers working in your profession! Archangel Haniel is helping bring about a massive change in the way corporate America operates. She shows me a vision of angels strategically placing healers around the world in leadership positions. When the time is right, all of these healers will be called up to the highest leadership positions within their respective companies or fields of work. With a network of corporate healer leaders in place, massive shifts will impact the way humanity works. People will be motivated to work with the vibrations of joy instead of fear. It's definitely a happy day to look forward to!

While it is Archangel Raziel who helps healers find their purpose, know their path, and what their God-given gifts are, it is Archangel Haniel who helps healers develop their gifts. She will help you:

1. Heighten your intuitive abilities
2. Understand how to protect your energy as an empath
3. Work through Egoic-Minded thoughts to trust your gifts
4. Develop your God-given talents to their fullest potential

Friend, this process can take years. For me, it took me the duration of my 20's just to accept that I was a healer. It took me my early 30's to awaken and develop my gifts and the last half of my thirties to begin working with people and building my business. I've been working with Archangel Haniel for over 20 years now, and I can tell you that she is the definition of grace, ease, and patience.

Oftentimes, a healer's Egoic Mind uses their empathic nature against them. The ego will push the healer to want to accomplish within one year what is actually meant to take that healer's entire lifetime to achieve. When the ego does this it's like you have the weight of the world on your shoulders and feel you have to do everything quickly now, now, now!

This happened to me a lot at the beginning. I would see visions of all that I was going to do. I remember being in my car after an energy healing class during my training and seeing a vision of how I would teach people to develop their spiritual gifts in my Angel Reiki School; I saw myself recording a series of videos for the program; I saw the podcast (but I didn't know what podcasts were at the time and mistakenly thought it to be a YouTube channel); I saw myself writing books and signing copies; and I saw all the things I will accomplish over the next 50–60+ years. However, my Egoic Mind would take the weight and magnitude of everything I am to do in this lifetime and place it as a ball of energy in front of my chest in my auric field. My Egoic Mind made me feel like I was behind or "late to the game" and that I was supposed to accomplish everything in my vision within a few short years. I felt like the weight of the world was on my shoulders. That's when I started working with Archangel Haniel. She came in early on to teach me how to release this energy and how to stop my Egoic Mind from sabotaging my progress.

When your Egoic Mind does this to you, Archangel Haniel is right there helping you see that you don't have to accomplish all of it right this moment or this year, and nor should you!

She helps you identify this trick of the ego and helps you see that your life is just as much about living in joy (enjoyment) as it is about creating. She helps your mind relax and accept that all you ever really have to do is be, and listen to your heart. Archangel Haniel says when we live life in joy, we allow our lives to unfold with ease and we listen to our hearts to take action steps forward with ease—that is what this life is all about, that is living this life with grace.

Archangel Haniel says one of the hardest parts about being a healer is trusting: trusting that you are in fact a healer, trusting that within you is a gift that will help others, trusting that you do, in fact, have God-given gifts and the ability to develop them to their fullest potential. It is your lack of trust that blocks you from fully living to your potential as a healer. Archangel Haniel helps you to trust by delivering God's miracles into your life as validation. She was there when Moses first heard the word of God, and she was there when he parted the Red Sea. She talks about what different men Moses was between those two moments. Archangel Haniel says Moses heard from God way before the burning bush, but he didn't believe. Archangel Haniel says God provides healers with the validation they need to believe in divine time. Moses hearing from God through the burning bush was the validation he needed to truly believe that everything else he'd heard up until that point was actually real! Archangel Haniel worked with Moses to develop his gift until he trusted with every ounce of his being that God would work miracles for him. She says that trust was what allowed Moses to part the Red Sea.

Archangel Haniel says God aims to work miracles in your life and through your life, too. She's working with you to trust and believe.

I've been teaching students how to develop their own unique God-given gifts in my Angel Reiki School since 2017. I know that after reading about Archangel Haniel, your first instinct will be to go to her, ask her to reveal your spiritual gifts to you, and teach you how to use them. You must understand that that is like asking God to make you a neurosurgeon right this moment. Many people's Egoic Minds will say, "I want to know what my spiritual gifts are and I want to use them right away!"

Friend, it just doesn't work like that: you have got to do the work.

To truly develop your gifts, you must learn a healing modality. You may, perhaps, be able to work with Archangel Haniel and your Spirit Team and have them help you open to your gifts over time without any outside training. However, that process unfolds much more slowly over decades, and takes more time than is needed. When you invest in yourself by taking a course and learning a healing modality, your learning rate is greatly accelerated because you're learning from teachers who've been through this before. Instead of having to make mistake after mistake in order to learn, you're paying someone to teach you the mistakes they've learned along the way, skipping years of research and starting where the most advanced teachers left off. The gift is that most times you get to go further than they did!

If you find Archangel Haniel encouraging you to work with a teacher, this is why! Archangel Haniel and Archangel Uriel channeled the Angel Reiki School through me for you. Unlike other programs out there that only teach you one method of healing, like energy work, the Angel Reiki School teaches you about your many spiritual gifts. You'll learn how those gifts work together and how Archangel Haniel is working with you to create your own healing business or birth healing creations into this world. If you go through another program, be sure they're not only teaching you energy healing. You want a program that opens you to your many God-given gifts and helps you develop them all!

You can connect with Archangel Haniel by getting into Oneness, asking her the following questions and writing down what comes to you:

1. Archangel Haniel, in what ways am I called to be a healer in this lifetime? (Remember this comes in more clearly during your training, when you sign up for the Angel Reiki School).

2. What training would you suggest that I receive so that I do not have to start from scratch and learn everything on my own?

3. What action steps would you have me take this week, this month, this year?

4. Archangel Haniel, what signs, colors or numbers do you use to communicate with me in my life? How will I know when you are around?

ARCHANGEL CHAMUEL

This life is meant to be shared with family and friends. Archangel Chamuel always says our relationships are the biggest gift in our life. If you disagree, close your eyes for a moment and imagine how lonely, isolating, and unfun it would be if you were the only human on Earth. It is our relationships with our partners, children, parents, siblings, extended family, and friends that make this life what it is. By caring deeply for other people we experience love, joy, and bliss.

Archangel Chamuel helps us navigate every relationship in our lives, new and old. He says relationships are a mirror that allow us to see ourselves so that we can grow as individuals. Through our relationships, we see what we don't know and we learn from it. From my college bestie's caring and thoughtful gestures towards me, I learned to be a more caring, thoughtful person myself. From my daughter, I learned to not pigeonhole someone into being what I need them to be, but to let them be free to soar on the path of their choosing. From my husband, I learned what it is to feel true, unconditional love and support. And because he loves me so well, it's taught me how to both accept more love, and love others better.

Through my work with Archangel Chamuel, I've learned that relationships are also about our growth as human beings. Maya Angelou said, "Do the best you can until you know better. Then when you know better, do better." This quote perfectly sums up how we grow through relationships in our lives. We grow up doing things one way, the way our parents taught us, and our parents did the best they could with what they had. But meeting other people is a gift! Like a mirror, relationships reflect us back to ourselves and allow us to grow and evolve by doing better, once we learn better. In this way, Archangel Chamuel is not only helping you navigate the complexities of relationships, but also navigate your relationship with yourself as well. Through our relationships with ourselves and others we learn about love. We experience the love we are as souls and from our human perspective, we learn how to be love and radiate love to all we meet.

Archangel Chamuel says it is our expectations of ourselves and others that often cause the most pain and growth. I held a belief for most of my life that I was supposed to be perfect. As a result, I expected others to be perfect as well. I had to learn that expectation was a lie from my Egoic Mind that could not be achieved. When I was first married, I had an expectation that my husband could read my mind and magically do all the things I was thinking without me actually verbalizing them. Again, I had to learn that expectation was a sabotaging trick of my Egoic Mind that could not be achieved. When we learn to question our expectations of ourselves and others in relationships, we work through a lot of Egoic Mind tricks, and learn to hold space for the flawed humanness of others. Isn't that what true unconditional love really is?

Another way Archangel Chamuel works with us is on our relationships with loved ones in Heaven. It is a misconceived notion that when someone we love passes away, our relationship with them is over: it is not over. It's simply the beginning of a new type of relationship. When my dad passed away (and I began hearing from him before becoming aware of his passing), I worked with Archangel Chamuel (and teachers on Earth) to learn how to communicate with him multiple times a day and hear the guiding words he whispered back to me. I learned to ask for specific signs and believe in those signs as validation that my dad's presence in my life was stronger than ever. Friend, Archangel Chamuel will help you to develop a deep connection with your loved ones on the Other Side as well! All you have to do is ask him!

Archangel Chamuel helps bring new relationships into your life as well. If you are looking for a romantic partner, new friend, or group of friends, ask Archangel Chamuel to bring the right people into your life for your benefit and theirs! Then be patient and watch Archangel Chamuel work miracles in your life, in divine time!

Friend, it's time for you to connect with Archangel Chamuel in Automatic Writing. Get into Oneness, and ask Archangel Chamuel to spend time with you. Here are some questions you can ask:

1. What is the lesson I am to learn in my relationship with _____?

2. How can I support the people I love more?

3. Is there a relationship I've neglected that you'd like me to pay more attention to?

4. Do I have unrealistic expectations within my relationship with _____? If so, how can I reframe that expectation?

5. What about myself is being mirrored back to me through my current relationships?

6. I would love a (insert one: romantic relationship or best friend or group of friends), can you help bring the right people into my life in divine time?

7. Archangel Chamuel, what signs, colors, or numbers do you use to communicate with me in my life? How will I know when you are around?

ARCHANGEL AZRAEL

Friend, Archangel Azrael always steps forward to work in my sessions when a client is at the end of a long life themselves or grieving the loss of a loved one. I've learned so much from Archangel Azrael about what it's like to pass from this life to the Other Side. It is not scary, but it is truly one of the most beautiful, peaceful processes for the person passing. It's so important that we begin to talk about this more because it would help us in our grief and our final transition!

There are two very different energies when it comes to passing away. For some, their passing is sudden and unexpected. For others, there is time to say goodbye and there is a conscious release of energy that must occur. Let's talk about the latter first.

What ties your energy to this Earth? Energetically, it's as if people walk around with roots coming out of their feet going down deeply into the Earth. Our roots are our passions, the spirit and excitement we have about being here and living this life; this energy grounds us and keeps us here. When a person is at the end of a long life, they must release their root energy by bringing it up from the ground, and making peace with leaving the only home they're conscious of, the people they've long been responsible for, and the obligations that gave them a sense of self. They have to make peace with the question, "Who am I, if I'm no longer a human on this Earth?"

When working with souls who are at the end of a long life, Archangel Azrael will show me that some souls are ready to go. It's like they say, "God, I've lived a long life. I'm so grateful for every moment, but I'm ready to go home. Please take me when you're ready." It is an easy, peaceful transition.

Other souls fear the death process because they don't understand what the Other Side is like or they fear having a conversation with a soul on the Other Side, whom they do not want to face. I've worked with many clients who were unfaithful to their partners in this lifetime and kept it a secret. Some clients were at the end of their long lives, their spouses already in Heaven, and they did not want to cross over because they feared their partners knew what they had done. Their shame and regret kept them from a peaceful passing, but no one in Heaven wants that. They're just ecstatic to be with us fully and wholly again! They want your passing to be peaceful. Still these souls' fear creates a kind of double-dutch energy. One minute they're ready to leave, the next minute their energy is rooted back into this Earth and they refuse to go. This type of passing can happen over the course of several years and the back-and-forth energy can be difficult on families. Archangel Azrael is always there to help that soul forgive themselves and finally transition.

It's easier to work with clients who are fearful of crossing over because they don't know what the Other Side is like, or perhaps they wonder if Heaven really exists. For these clients, Archangel Azrael will come in and speak to them at length about what the Other Side is really like. The Other Side is not one singular place the way that Earth is; it is infinite and made up of multiple different layers and realms.

Spirit finds it funny that we humans assume the Other Side is not material as this world is. They say in Heaven, we have everything that we have on Earth and so much more. On the Other Side we have homes, family, friends, travel, experiences, food, and drink. Sometimes a loved one will come into a session and show me a framed photo they have hanging in their heavenly home. I'll describe the photo to my clients and most report they have the same photo hanging in their home here. Our loved ones do this to show how meaningful our connection to them is even from the Other Side.

Archangel Azrael will often show my clients all there is to the Other Side. In Heaven, there is a palace where everyone has their own home, which I call "Home Base." There is a place to travel and see everything you did not get to see on Earth (or everything you want to see again); there is a place to go and learn; there is a place to be of service and help those still living on Earth. Archangel Azrael has shown me Heaven is more beautiful than we can imagine. The colors are more vibrant and radiant. At Home Base, all the souls from your soul family (made up of every lifetime you've lived) all have homes right next to one another in the same *subdivision*, if you will. Keep in mind, the physical laws of Earth do not apply in Heaven.

Some people love the mountains, some love the ocean, some love farm country. They say our souls are together at Home Base, and to be there is like each soul being able to look out of their own eyes and see the scenery they love. This means that if my home is next to my dad's on the Other Side and he loves the mountains, but I love the beach, we can be next to one another and he will see mountains and I will see the beach while we spend time together in the same place.

Another piece that is vital (although difficult) for our human minds to understand is our omnipresence. In a session, Archangel Azrael will often explain to a grieving wife or mother how our souls are still with our loved ones who've passed on. He explains it like this: You are made in the likeness and image of God in that your soul is omnipresent just as God is omnipresent. What does that mean? Have you ever heard the term "Higher Self?" Your Higher Self is an omnipresent piece of your soul that is always in Heaven, even while you are living a human life on Earth. To put it plainly—you are in two places at once (if not more). You are here now in this physical body on Earth and you are also in Heaven experiencing a conscious existence there, at the same time. You don't remember it because that's what it is to be human. We lose all memory of our soul-self and go on a life journey to awaken, remember, and return to it!

When my dad passed away and went to Heaven, my human self was here on Earth grieving. However, my dad was greeted by my Higher Self and he gets to spend time with me regularly over there. His relationship with me from Heaven is now two-fold. He stays connected to my human self by sending signs and teaching me to communicate more with him. Yet he has a full relationship, daily, with my Higher Self who is in Heaven with him. It is the same with you and your loved ones. There is a space where you are with them fully, always!

For those who pass suddenly or unexpectedly, the only difference is they do not have to do the work of releasing their energy from being rooted into Earth. In the year and months leading up to their passing, I do not believe their human self is conscious of what is coming, but their Higher Self knows. Those who listen to the podcast know my dad passed away suddenly from a heart attack while hiking in Colorado in 2015. Nine months prior to his passing, I began receiving signs encouraging me to reconnect with him. After his passing, I was told he was receiving those same signs and felt called to reconnect with me too. I know that Archangel Azrael, my dad's Higher Self, and my Higher Self were all pushing us from Heaven to mend things before his unexpected departure, but both of us were too prideful to make the call.

Archangel Azrael works with you when you lose someone close. From everything I've experienced and seen when it comes to death, what I know is this: It is harder to lose someone than to go through the death process yourself. I've worked with hundreds of grieving widows and every time, Archangel Azrael shows me they have one of two choices: either refuse to move forward or surrender and accept the journey forward. Many people cannot see a clear path forward after a great loss. If that is you, please know that Archangel Azrael is always there leading you through (we'll dig deeper into this next, when we discuss Archangel Jeremiel).

Archangel Azrael has taught me to understand where a person is emotionally by feeling their energy. On a normal day of your life your energy feels like you are swimming in the gentle rolling waves of the ocean. When you are grieving, your energy feels like you are trying to stay afloat in the middle of the ocean during a hurricane, with ten foot waves constantly approaching and growing higher. Grief-energy is some of the most difficult energy to navigate, and you cannot do it alone. You must surround yourself with Earth angels to support you and call on Archangel Azrael to ease your pain.

Connect with Archangel Azrael today, by getting into Oneness and asking him to spend time with you. Archangel Azrael wants you to do something different this time. Sit in Oneness for three minutes, then ask yourself, "What questions do I have for Archangel Azrael?" I want you to write those questions below and record the response that he gives you.

_____

_____

_____

_____

_____

_____

_____

_____

_____

_____

_____

_____

_____

_____

_____

_____

_____

_____

_____

ARCHANGEL JEREMIEL

Archangel Jeremiel and Archangel Azrael often work together in helping souls cross from this life to the next. Whereas, Archangel Azrael helps souls release their energy from this world, Archangel Jeremiel meets the soul as soon as their energy lifts from their body. Archangel Jeremiel's presence is peace, love, and ease. As soon as you feel Archangel Jeremiel's presence you feel comforted, safe, and at home.

Archangel Jeremiel's job is to oversee a soul's entire transition from the moment they leave the physical body until consciousness is fully reintegrated on the Other Side. He's shown me the process:

When your soul is thrust out of the physical body, there is no pain, no fear, and no low emotion. You are greeted by members of your soul family and angels who make you feel at home. There is a sense of the greatest love you've ever felt (one you never want to leave) and an immediate fusing back into your Higher Self consciousness. When your human consciousness fuses back into your Higher Self consciousness there is all knowing. It's a remembrance of every detail of your life plan, every lifetime you've ever lived, every moment of your existence. You return to the essence of your soul and you are again pure love, joy, peace, bliss, ease, and grace. You are fully and completely detached from your Egoic Mind. Because your soul is omnipresent, you are now omnipresent again too. It's as if parts of you simultaneously move in different directions to carry out different tasks.

1. A part of you goes home to a party in Heaven where everyone is waiting to celebrate the life you just lived. As I mentioned before, because your soul is omnipresent your Higher Self remains in Heaven even while you're living on Earth. So when a soul passes, they're greeted at this heavenly party, not just by all their loved ones who've already passed away, but also the higher selves of every family member still living a human life. At this party we feel so joy-filled to be home, surrounded by everyone we love. After this party, this part of our souls goes to our physical home on the Other Side where all souls from our soul family live in the same place (let's call it the same heavenly subdivision). When I feel souls enter this place, it's a feeling of collapse into relaxation. Like when you get to a destination on vacation, plop onto the hotel bed and say, "Ahhhhhhhhhh, I made it!"

2. At the same time, a part of your soul stays back on Earth to manage the energy of your passing. Whether your passing is unexpected or not, we always get time to fully say goodbye. For example, I was at work when I heard the news that my dad passed away (a full month

after he had passed). I went home mid-day to an empty house. With no one around to hear me, I screamed as loud as I could and went off on my dad. I ranted and swore at him out loud. I remember screaming at him over and over, "You left and you didn't even fucking fix things here. You left everything broken. You were supposed to fix it! You told me you'd fix it. You didn't fix it! You can't go!" My heart had broken into a thousand pieces. I felt immense grief and yet, I was beyond pissed, infuriated that I never received what I needed from him. At the time, I felt I never would.

I remember hearing my dad talking back to me as I was shouting at him. It felt like he was three feet higher than me, but his energy was barricaded behind a glass-like wall. I heard, "I hear everything you're saying, and I'm going to fix things. I promise I'll fix things not just for you, but everyone I hurt. I'm so sorry, Julie."

Not all souls have this exchange. Many are so proud of the relationships they developed here and come through to you after their passing with beautiful goodbyes and signs to let you know they're okay. It's important for you to use this time with them if you can. This is where Archangel Azrael comes back in. As I mentioned in the earlier chapter on Azrael, everyone experiences grief differently.

For some, the closeness in energy after a loved one has just passed is a wonderful opportunistic moment to talk to them and say the things you need to say, feel their presence, hear them speak to you through your own internal dialogue, establish signs and begin to feel what it's like to communicate with them in this new way. Many people use this time to write their loved one a letter and begin dabbling in Automatic Writing. Others feel too much grief right after a loved one has passed and cannot feel their loved one's presence until this grief has subsided. Friend, there is no right way to go about this. You take it as it comes, minute by minute if you have to, and ask for Archangel Azrael to guide you.

3. A part of your soul serves on the Spirit Teams of your loved ones still living on Earth. It's as if you have a radio dial set to the station of each of your loved ones who are still living, and you're always dialed into what is going on and what is coming up. Our Spirit Teams get together as a group at times, and they're always there for us when we call on them. They assure you that because they are omnipresent they are able to be everywhere all at once and they plead with you to please call on them for all things small, medium, and large. You are not bothering them, they want to help!

4. A part of your soul goes to your life review. Some people fear they are going to stand in front of God or their loved ones and be judged, but this isn't how it works. In Heaven, your soul is love, joy, peace, bliss, ease, and grace, and so it cannot hurt another soul. Yet, as human beings, it may be our unintentional action or lack of action that does cause others pain in this lifetime. Some say in this life review you judge yourself, but this is also incorrect. It's not a judgement, it is the reciprocation of energy.

Looking back at your life, you'll see how you took actions that hurt people, you took actions that helped people, and in some cases you chose not to take any action at all, which also impacted people. All of your actions, positive or negative, impacted both individual souls and the greater collective consciousness made up of all living souls. There are times when our actions do not just impact one person, but also others they know or their future lineage. Our life review is a simulation in which we live from the bodies and minds of the people we hurt for the duration of their pain. In feeling their pain, the pain we caused as our human selves, we take back the pain we caused and undo our harm. In our life review, we will undo every harm we ever caused both big and small. It's how we learn. Most people are in and out of their life review in a snap, but people like Hitler and his associates are still there "living" through every pain they ever caused and everyone impacted (whether that be at the time or Jewish relatives who are still impacted by his crimes today)—this is karma. We do not roll over our karma from one life to another. All karma is worked out either in our current lifetime or in our life review.

This gives us freedom to begin each lifetime with a clean slate.

It's important to note that we can work out our karma here and now, in our current lifetime. It's one of the most powerful energies in the Alcoholics Anonymous program where they tell you to ask forgiveness from everyone you ever hurt. This is a start. Archangel Jeremiel and Archangel Azrael have shown me that you can work your karma out more quickly here on Earth than in your life review on the Other Side, because doing your work here sets an example that others can replicate. This is why some people are canonized as Saints. Many are examples of exemplary beings that the rest of humanity can look up to. When we work out our karma here on Earth it counts for more because others can see us right our wrongs. When someone sees you make a positive change in your life and humbly ask for forgiveness, you're showing them what is possible in their own life. You're helping create positive change in the collective consciousness by impacting individuals.

This is what is needed—public displays in which we humbly right our wrongs and take responsibility. Doing this raises the vibration of the planet.

All of the 4 parts happen simultaneously and Archangel Jeremiel is there to guide your soul through every step of the way. If you've lost a loved one and need help connecting with their energy, I recommend going to both Archangel Jeremiel and Archangel Azrael and asking for their assistance. Both will help you establish a relationship from both sides of the veil.

Connect with Archangel Jeremiel by getting into Oneness and asking him to spend time with you. Again sit in Oneness, then ask yourself, "What questions do I have for Archangel Jeremiel?" I want you to write those questions below and record the response that he gives you.

_____

_____

_____

_____

_____

_____

_____

_____

_____

_____

_____

_____

_____

_____

ANGEL
COMMUNICATION
Part 2: Week One

If you're in the Angel Membership,
go to the Angel Communication Part 2 course
(in the folder titled *A Year With Your Angels*):

☐ Watch the following videos:
   ☐ **Archangel Uriel**
   ☐ **Archangel Jophiel**
   ☐ **Archangel Metatron**
   ☐ **Archangel Zadkiel**

ARCHANGEL URIEL

Archangel Uriel is one of many angels that assists healers. Again, when I say "healer," I mean any soul who is here to serve humanity in some capacity, regardless of the line of work. Any person who serves the betterment of the collective is a healer. Healers work with many archangels to become who they were meant to be in this life:

1. Archangel Raziel helps healers understand their purpose, their path and identify their God-given spiritual gifts
2. Archangel Haniel helps healers to develop and trust their spiritual gifts.
3. Archangel Uriel helps healers fully develop their spiritual gifts, build a business (in any line of work that best serves the collective in raising the vibration of Earth), and also teach what they've learned

Archangel Uriel is an archangel who's been seen as both male and female. I've seen her as both but refer to her here with female pronouns because that is the way she comes through to me most often. Feel free to refer to Uriel in the way he/she comes through to you.

In order for humanity to heal on a deeper level and come to a place of peace, Archangel Uriel says new pathways of healing must be developed. She says you can view it as "healing highways." Archangel Uriel shows me a vision of 7.5+ billion people on the planet and she says before there were only a few known highways of "healing" like yoga, hypnotherapy, meditation, Reiki Energy Healing, sound therapy, psychic mediumship, and more. She says humanity has changed in that it needs new "healing highways" in order for all souls to experience an awakening.

In meditation, Archangel Uriel has taken me back to the 1990's to oversee how past healing training sessions were run. She shows me that people were often told to "stay in their lane," and if they were not doing things in a precise way, they were rebuked or shamed by the healing community. Archangel Uriel shows this energy completely shifted in 2011. Right now, healers are being called to bridge different forms of healing with what Spirit is showing them. What does this look like? Within you may be an idea for a healing business that is different from all others. This idea is with you because you are to create it over time. Archangel Uriel says your gift is not supposed to look like anyone else's. Your gift is unique to you because it's what you need to serve souls that you're here to help!

Here's what Archangel Uriel needs you to see: Imagine yourself serving other souls here on Earth. How many souls are you able to help in your lifetime? 10,000? 100,000? 1 million? 1 billion? More? Ask Spirit to show you a number and allow it to come to you. Now, take that number and see that many orbs behind your back. Those are the higher selves of souls you are here to help in this lifetime. Their energy is behind you, pushing you to become who you will be because when you become that healer, you influence their path and shift their trajectory. Archangel Uriel says that you're part of a group of healers here who must take action because your path influences other souls' life paths.

Many would ask the question, "So how do I become a healer?" The better question is, "What is a healer?" because it will bring you a better understanding of your path. A soul either is a healer or not. It's part of the essence of who you are. Healers are molded, shaped and sculpted. Yes, a person is born a healer, but that does not give them what they need to lead. A healer is sculpted from their life experiences; the healing modalities they learn and become certified in; working with thousands of people to deeply understand their pain/struggles. A healer is so empathic that they feel everything that is coming before it arrives to the collective. A healer synthesizes all that information and delivers Spirit's messages to humanity through teachings, videos, social media posts, books, podcasts, YouTube channels, and new upcoming technology—that's what a healer is. When every healer rises to this calling, the 7.5+ billion souls on Earth will have all the "healing highways" they need to heal collectively and shift the planet. So how are we going to get there?

Have you ever heard the saying, "born from fire?" Healers are born from fire and the work it takes to grow into the person you are to be. Healers experience things from a different perspective than the general population:

1. Healers feel or go through things days, weeks, months, or years before the collective does. This process gives them the tools needed to guide the collective through a massive energy.

2. When healers compare their lives to others, they often feel as though they've been through more in their life than others have. And many times that's true because Spirit says we cannot help others heal if we have not lived something ourselves. Spirit will place experiences in our paths that allow us to learn first hand. I learned how to heal from moving every few years as a kid; my parents' divorce; losing my dad; raising a medically complex child; overcoming a rocky time in my marriage to building a life I love with him; starting a successful business from scratch; I learned how to heal from suicidal ideation, and entirely rebuild my life. Your life experiences make you the healer you need to be in order to reach the souls you're here to help.

3. Your life experiences are different from your experiences as a healer. When you work with thousands of people each year, you begin to see common energy threads. It's as if a majority of humanity is struggling with the same thing at the same time and you can feel it. Spirit provides you with this insight as a healer so that you can help the majority with the issue at hand. Becoming certified in a healing modality is a necessary step for traditional healers, but it doesn't stop there. It is your experience working with your clients (or souls you're here to serve) that shows you what messages they need most in their lives. You become a better and better healer with each soul you serve.

4. Why do I say that becoming certified in a healing modality is a necessity? Because it is your vehicle by which you process information. I learned energy healing as my modality and doing so opened me up. I learned to feel energy and read into what different energies meant. When I began my training, Spirit began to work with me more because through my freewill, I was saying, "Yes, I'm ready to do this! God, I'm ready to work for you. Show me the way!" Everytime I practiced on a volunteer, that person's Spirit Team was right there with messages! I wouldn't have known the full breadth of my capabilities if I had not gone through a training program.

When I completed my training program, I knew I had what I needed to begin serving. Archangel Uriel often says healers are "born from fire" because we are leaders trailblazing a new path where there was nothing before. Sometimes it is a lonely path because only we see the vision of our future that Spirit is giving us and others think we're "crazy" when we discuss it with them. After completing your training, you may have visions of the work you will be doing 10, 15, 20, 40 years down the road. Trust the positive visions your angels show you. You're seeing them for a reason.

Archangel Uriel channeled the Angel Reiki School through me because she said there are not enough programs available that help you focus on developing all your gifts, not just the healing modality itself. If you're looking for a training program, check out my Angel Reiki School at theangelmedium.com/angel-reiki-school for details or to enroll.

If you are a healer, Archangel Uriel is working with you through every life experience you have. She's helping you heal so you can replicate what she shows you and teach others to heal in the same way. Call on Archangel Uriel to help you fine-tune your spiritual gifts, to better understand the messages you receive, and turn up the volume on hearing Spirit's messages. If you are a teacher or teach in some capacity in the future, ask Archangel Uriel to give you the words the world needs to hear.

Spend some time with Archangel Uriel. First, get into Oneness. Connect with her energy and ask her the following questions and any others you may have:

1. Am I a healer? If so, in what way? (Remember this comes in more clearly during your training, when you sign up for the Angel Reiki School).

2. How am I here to serve humanity?

3. How can I best develop my gifts further?

4. What have I experienced in my life that's prepared me for my journey as a healer?

5. Will I teach other healers one day?

6. Archangel Uriel, what signs, colors or numbers do you use to communicate with me in my life? How will I know when you are around?

_____

_____

_____

_____

_____

_____

_____

_____

_____

_____

_____

_____

_____

ARCHANGEL JOPHIEL

I touched on this previously, but I want to go into it more closely here because this is Archangel Jophiel's work. Your soul can never be broken, damaged, or diminished in any way, but your spirit is different from your soul. Your spirit is your strength, confidence, and passion to live this life and continue moving forward with excitement! While Archangel Gabrielle helps you return to your spirit through your joy, Archangel Jophiel takes over from there and helps your spirit become strong, confident, and resilient.

Remember back to the pages on Archangel Michael that referenced the cartoons we grew up watching where the devil would be on one side and an angel would be talking on the Other Side? Together Archangel Jophiel, Archangel Michael, and Archangel Gabrielle hover on your shoulder and encourage you not to attach to Egoic Mind thoughts, but to listen to your intuition instead. Archangel Jophiel is a strong, compassionate cheerleader in her approach (though her demeanor is more like Rocky Balboa's boxing coach than an actual "rah-rah" cheerleader).

Archangel Jophiel only sees your potential and the path to build up your confidence. I was working with a client the other day who said, "I'm 42 years old and I keep feeling like I'm going to get passed over for a promotion and it's going to go to someone ten years younger." Archangel Jophiel came in and said, "The 30-somethings in your office feel the same about you! They feel that you've been waiting for the promotion and it's yours!" She says you can reframe any thought to see it through a more positive lens, but it's deeper than just reframing a thought one time. Because 80% of your 12,000–60,000 thoughts a day are negative, and 95% of those are repetitive, your thoughts will either hold your back or propel you forward. Either one you choose will shape your entire life. Archangel Jophiel helps you not just think positively for one day, week, or month, but she helps you create real long-lasting change within your life that truly stays with you, by rewiring your mind.

Your thoughts create emotions and feelings within your body. When your thoughts hold you back from something you want to attain, it's because they've filled you with fear that inhibits your ability to move forward for a time. My Egoic Mind will do this thing where it compares me to other people on social media. Do you ever look at social media, see someone else's posts and think, "I'm not good enough. Why do I even bother?" Between 2008–2018, these thoughts within my head would cause me to feel negatively about myself. A thought would begin repeating in my mind, "I'm not worthy. Maybe if I were skinnier, prettier, or smarter… but I'm not and I never will be." I would feel bad for myself and any progress I had made was out the window. I'd feel bad for a week, sometimes even a month before I'd find my confidence again. We often talk about Archangel Jophiel as inspiring creatives with beautiful ideas, but before a person can run with those ideas, they must be confident in themselves; and that requires us to work on our Egoic Mind with Archangel Jophiel.

Working with Archangel Jophiel woke me up to a self-sabotaging pattern within myself, in 2018 and she taught me to break free of it by:

1. **Looking at my priorities and releasing fear**: When I'm paralyzed with fear, it doesn't help anyone. I'm not in a place of servitude because I'm just trying to survive, myself. When I take the spotlight off of myself, I ask God to humble me and I ask to be a tool that They can work through. I pick myself up, dust myself off, and get back to work.

2. **Rewiring my mind**: Archangel Jophiel says that worry happens when our minds create "mountains from molehills." She says the way to overcome this is by zooming out and concentrating on the bigger picture. Think about it this way: for decades I knew I would write a book but my Egoic Mind would tell me, "This is big! It has to be perfect!" I would stress so much that I would be paralyzed with fear and the book never got written. Archangel Jophiel said, "No! You're not just an author, you're going to be a book publisher one day, run conferences, and touch more lives than you can imagine. The book isn't the whole pie, it's just a tiny slice. Don't stress about the book, focus on the bigger publishing company and let the book fall into place." So that's what I did, and this book was channeled over the three months that followed. Whenever you feel fear, zoom out to see the larger picture, and watch as what you were stressing about falls into place!

3. **Not caring who likes me**: I am a people pleaser through and through! It used to drive me nuts when someone didn't like me. I would think to myself, "Why? I never did anything to them," and I'd do everything possible to change their opinion of me. Archangel Jophiel taught me the phrase, "Fuck it." She taught me to accept that another person's opinion of me truly has nothing to do with me. It is no reflection of who I am as a person, so why waste my time on them? Today, I reserve my time for my supporters. Those who uplift and encourage me in the work I do. Don't waste time trying to convince everyone to like you. Focus on the people who love your message!

Working with Archangel Jophiel is a journey, not an event. It's taken me years of practice not to allow my Egoic Mind to paralyze me with fear. There are times when I have to be extremely firm with my Egoic Mind. When a thought is with me that I don't want to think, Archangel Jophiel taught me to speak back to it within my mind and say, "No, I'm not going there. No, I'm not taking the bait. I don't want to think that." I'll feed myself a thought that I *do* want to think instead. If my Egoic Mind tells me that I'm going to end up having diabetes in 20 years like other family members, I'll speak back to it and visualize myself at 90 years old, working out with weights, feeling great, driving, being more mentally "with it" and physically fit than ever.

Archangel Jophiel says this process is vital to developing the strength, confidence, and courage needed to birth our creations into this world. Many creators and artists fear that they only get one or two really great ideas in this life. They spend all their time perfecting those few ideas, but Archangel Jophiel says that's not how creation energy works. When you are an artist, a writer, a fashion designer, a video game creator, a marketing genius, or other creator, divine ideas want to be birthed through you one after the other. Divine ideas are limitless. The only thing that can limit them is your attachment to Egoic-Minded thoughts, which hold you back. Archangel Jophiel will place divine, inspired thought in you and build up your confidence so that you are able to reach your fullest potential in this lifetime.

It's time for you to connect with Archangel Jophiel. Get into Oneness and ask her to spend time with you. Then ask Archangel Jophiel:

1. What creations want to be birthed through me at this time or in the near future?

2. What small details am I stressing over?

3. What is the bigger picture of what I am to create that I'm not seeing right now?

4. Am I a people pleaser? Am I worried about what other people are going to think of me? How can I see this differently?

5. Archangel Jophiel, what signs, colors or numbers do you use to communicate with me in my life? How will I know when you are around?

6. Is there anything else you'd like me to know?

ARCHANGEL METATRON

When I first heard about Archangel Metatron, I was weirded-out by the fact that his name sounds very *woo-woo*, but the more I worked with him I found his energy to be just like any other angel. Today, I love working with him and find that he works miracles all the time in my life. I know you'll find the same!

Remember in the chapter on guardian angels I was telling you about the TV show I'd once seen where it showed an infinite number of energy lines crossing back and forth representing the freewill choices of each person? In my sessions, Archangel Metatron shows me how this actually works. He says because humans have freewill, there is an infinite number of options available to us at all times. Archangel Metatron shows me that with each choice we are either moving in the direction of our soul's path or not. When we make a choice that is not in alignment with our soul's path, new energy lines are instantaneously formed that will help guide us back to God and our soul's path, if we so choose.

That does not mean we will take this new path. Following what resonates with us and what feels in alignment with us is always our choice. As you can imagine, with 7.5+ billion people on the planet these energy lines are constantly changing. But what Archangel Metatron wants you to hear is that you cannot be lost from God. Anytime you make a choice that is not aligned with God's vision, your guardian angels and the Cherubs work to instantly create new energetic lines or options to bring you back home to your soul self.

Archangel Metatron is both the keeper of God's vision for this world and the one who ensures all small details are executed on time. It is a massive job and he doesn't do it alone. Archangel Metatron ensures this infinite number of energy lines is constantly upholding God's vision for humanity and he knows how every choice you make will impact both the collective 7.5+ billion people as a whole and on an individual level. He sees how every small part fits into God's big overview vision, but it is the Cherubs and your guardian angels who take this vision and run with it! The Cherubs instantly draw new lines of energy from you back to God every time you fall off your path. Your guardian angels are the wind at your back and the whispers in your ear asking you to turn back to God.

Archangel Metatron shows me this is where sacred geometry comes in. He says when you walk this life in alignment and resonance with God's vision, the lines of energy of your actions form a sacred symbol that the angels can see from above. However, this symbol is not just a "symbol," it is much more and you can feel this for yourself. When you spend time in meditation with sacred geometry symbols, you can feel the palpable, high vibrational Oneness frequency they emit. Archangel Metatron says this works in a similar way to a sonar system. When you walk in alignment with God you are walking in line with your personal sacred geometry shape which is why alignment feels good to you. But when you step out of alignment, you step out of your shape and you can feel that too.

There is a second function to all of this. Archangel Metatron says when you walk in alignment with the lines and shapes of your life, your shape fits into the bigger shape that is God's vision. The shapes interlock to form a protective bubble/force around you. Do not see this as a bubble around you exclusively—it is bigger than that. This bubble is a protective shield, at the same level as the atmosphere. Archangel Metatron says with this network, you are protected anywhere you go on Earth and automatically connected to others who are on their paths (in their sacred geometry shapes) as well.

This network is not meant to be seen, it is meant to be felt—and it feels like Oneness. Archangel Metatron says this connects you to the possibility of miracles because you are dialed into God's network. Call it a miracle network. Archangel Metatron says prayer is effective because it taps into the miracle network of all other aligned souls. Think of it like this: Did you know some corporations have a system where employees can "bank" their sick days? When one of the employees must take leave due to a severe illness or injury, the "sick bank" is a resource which allows the person to take additional paid sick days. This is a blessing because the person can focus on getting well and not worry about returning to work for a paycheck. Archangel Metatron says our collective prayers activate the miracle network and tap into an infinite, limitless "energy bank" of divine energy. If the prayer aligns with God's vision, miracles can occur.

Archangel Metatron wants to clarify two things: The bank is infinite abundance (because it is God), and the more we pray the more palpable God's vibration on Earth is (Earth's vibration rises). The bank can never be depleted so you don't need to limit yourself to only asking for help with the big things. In fact, the more you ask for help with everything, small, medium and large, the more energy goes into the bank and the more God's energy is felt on Earth. Your prayers don't just help you. Your prayers, even for yourself, help others too.

It is said that Archangel Metatron keeps a record of everything that happens here on Earth in the Book of Life. I view this, not as a written language, but as a *vibrational language*. The infinite energetic lines of our freewill choices hold vibrational frequency and all information of everything everywhere in this life is recorded.

Archangel Metatron will help you bring the vibration of ease into your life. There are a lot of people who say you don't have to work "hard" to be successful and they're right. When you take any step in your life your energy is in motion. When your energy is in motion it is a mixture of your freewill, your intention, your prayers (or co-creation energy), your action steps and the level of Oneness you're tapped into. Anything you do in life can be done in Oneness or from the push, anxiety, and stress of the Egoic Mind. The choice is yours.

Archangel Metatron says, "Remember, you can never be lost. You can never not know what to do. The answer is always there with you through Oneness." When you go to make a decision, "Do I go this way? Or that way?" sit with both options and see which vibrates at the frequency of Oneness. You will know which option puts you in Oneness because you will feel alignment and resonance. When we think, "Yeah, I feel the Oneness in 'option A', but I really want 'option B'," we are moving against what resonates with us, choosing the will of our Egoic Mind (and we almost always wind up kicking ourselves for that decision).

Life doesn't have to be as hard or as difficult as we make it out to be. When we live in Oneness and follow the path God has laid on our hearts, we live in ease, grace, and bliss. Yes, we still have challenges but despite them, when we follow our hearts, what resonates with us, what feels in alignment then we live in Oneness and doing so is like living in Heaven on Earth.

I find that when I ask Archangel Metatron for help with everything, my life flows and things click into place that had once been frustrating. I am calm in times I would have otherwise been stressed. Sometimes, I ask Archangel Metatron to slow down time so I can complete everything I need to in a shorter period and he does! He helps me with my organization, time management and knowledge and it allows me to go further in life more quickly. You can call on Archangel Metatron to help with anything you need to accomplish your goals here on Earth.

Allow Archangel Metatron to help you live in Heaven on Earth, Oneness, and ease by connecting with his energy and asking the following questions. Remember to get into Oneness (if you aren't already simply from reading this chapter).

1. What parts of my life are in alignment and resonance with God's will?

2. What parts of my life are not in alignment and resonance with God's will?

3. How can I live in a more constant vibration of ease?

4. What would my life look like if I lived in flow, ease and Heaven on Earth more frequently?

5. When I make this change in my life will it positively impact the lives of those around me? How so?

6. Archangel Metatron, what signs, colors or numbers do you use to communicate with me in my life? How will I know when you are around?

7. Archangel Metatron, what else do I need to know?

_____

_____

_____

_____

_____

_____

_____

_____

_____

_____

_____

_____

_____

_____

_____

_____

_____

ARCHANGEL ZADKIEL

Archangel Metatron and Archangel Zadkiel's roles in your life work in tandem. While Archangel Metatron helps you to live a life of ease and Heaven on Earth, you cannot live in this energy without simultaneously holding the energy of surrender. Surrender is the energy of Archangel Zadkiel.

Surrender is different from releasing energy or letting things go. Surrender is much bigger. It is going to God intentionally and saying, "Your Will God, not mine. Lead me. My life is yours. I will be the tool. Show me what to do, and I'll do it."

In the previous chapters on Oneness, I told you about my awakening and how my entire life felt like it was falling apart but, here's what I didn't tell you: A few days after checking myself in at the hospital psych ward, an Earth angel psychiatrist helped me to realize I could not go back to the life I was living before. When I surrendered to this, it felt scary and beautifully freeing all at once. The life I had been living was dead and gone. I could not go back, and I was thankful I didn't have to live that life any longer—but by the grace of God I was still alive. I had a future to build and a new life to create.

Before building something new, I wanted to examine why the life I had just created fell apart. I thought back over the previous decade and all my choices and I realized I hadn't involved God in any of it, in a meaningful way, in a long time. Without God, the life I had built for me by me was built on the sand that is the Egoic Mind. I asked God to take the reins. I gave up control.

I forgave myself for getting it wrong and I surrendered my life to Their will, whatever that life would be.

Friend, at the time I was describing this part of my life to people by saying, "Metaphorically, I feel like I am walking a tightrope between two skyscrapers, except when I look down, there is no rope. A momentary zap of fear makes me feel as though I will plummet to the ground. But God asks me to take a blind step forward on the callings of my heart. As I do, the next piece of rope magically appears, and I am able to simply keep walking forward." There is a sense of nervousness not knowing the mysteries of my life that are coming, but it's also wildly exciting and fun. As Gabrielle Bernstein's famous book title says, "The Universe Has Your Back." I knew then that God had my back and always would.

I was once told by an auric reader that I would do this work one day (if I so chose). I was also told, "You are known in Heaven. God knows your name and you are always cared for. You will return to Heaven feeling fulfilled because you did everything your soul came here to do." When I surrendered, these words kept coming to me. And for the first time, I truly and completely believed them. When we surrender to the fact that the universe has our back, we realize all we ever have to do is just be by breathing, putting one foot in front of the other and continuing to exist.

I've found that surrender is really about communicating with God. So much of what you've read in this book about angels and how they are working with you ties into God's plan for you. How do you know what that plan is? You learn to distinguish between the voice of your Egoic Mind and the voice of your intuition. You learn to hear your intuition more clearly and trust it. Friend, I hope you don't expect yourself to get this overnight. Trusting your intuition requires you to rewire your brain and think differently, consistently, over a long period of time. When you learn to trust your intuition, you're not going to get it right every time. Surrender is a spiritual practice because it's something we have to do everyday. Surrender asks you to forgive yourself every time you backslide, pick yourself up, dust yourself off, and continue moving forward in trusting your inner wisdom. In a state of surrender, we are humbled and we happily "give the glory to God" because we've learned we don't want to walk this life alone. We want to walk the path God designed for us with God right by our sides.

Surrendering our lives to God's will doesn't absolve us from taking responsibility. In fact, it's just the opposite. Surrender means taking responsibility for being open, spending time with God, hearing what God wants for our lives and taking action steps forward based on Their will.

At any moment in your life, there is always an action step for you to take in order to work toward the purpose God gave you and the energy of that step is placed within you. It is a step that calls to you within your heart. You know this step through:

1. The four clairs (*your hearing, seeing, feeling and knowingness*).
2. Your daily spiritual practice.
3. Automatic Writing with God.
4. Holding Oneness.

Over time, as you surrender consistently (daily), you stop thinking as much from the Egoic Mind and trust your intuition, instead. As you do this, your Egoic Mind no longer has a hold over you, and cannot limit you or what you can achieve in this lifetime because you're no longer bound by limited thinking. Surrender opens you up to the infinite possibilities of the divine. It opens you up to God's abundance in all things—health, wealth, joy, love, peace—and a lifetime of miracles.

Archangel Zadkiel is patient and gives you the space and time you need to go through this process. It's time for you to connect with Archangel Zadkiel and ask for his help in surrendering, forgiving yourself, loving yourself more, and taking action toward God's vision for your life. Here are some questions you can ask him in Automatic Writing:

1. Have I fully surrendered? In what ways am I still trying to control my life?

2. How can I surrender more each day?

3. Have I forgiven myself for my past mistakes or do I need to work on forgiving myself? Archangel Zadkiel, please show me what I need to work on.

4. What would my life look like if I surrendered entirely?

5. Archangel Zadkiel, what signs, colors or numbers do you use to communicate with me in my life? How will I know when you are around?

6. Archangel Zadkiel, what else do I need to know?

_____

_____

_____

_____

_____

_____

_____

_____

_____

_____

_____

_____

ANGEL COMMUNICATION

Part 2: Week Two

If you're in the Angel Membership,
go to the Angel Communication Part 2 course
(in the folder titled *A Year With Your Angels*):

☐ Watch **Connecting With Your Loved Ones**.

☐ Listen to **Angel Meditation**.

CONNECTING WITH LOVED ONES IN HEAVEN

This chapter is a more abbreviated lesson in how to connect with your loved ones (which I teach in a more in-depth context in the Angel Membership), but your departed loved ones also wanted me to include it here because it is so important. The Angel Membership course goes much deeper and I hope you'll join us there to build a stronger connection with your loved ones on the Other Side by walking through the full year-long program *A Year With Your Angels*.

Omnipresence allows the souls of your loved ones on the Other Side to be with you at all times! Departed souls often get a kick out of us human beings thinking about Heaven because it is typically so far off from the truth! Heaven isn't a one dimensional space made of floaty clouds. Spirit has shown me there is a very real physical component to Heaven as well. Over there we have physical food, drink, clothes, cars, beaches to visit, mountains to climb, skills to learn and eons of time to spend with the souls we love. Despite all that, departed souls say there is nothing more important to them than the human life *you* are living now and ensuring you are okay at all times. You are their number one priority because what you're doing here in your life is important.

Your loved ones on the Other Side want you to build a relationship with them and by "relationship" they mean constant communication. It upsets your departed loved ones when you say, "I don't want to bother them for the small stuff. I'll only ask for help with the bigger things." They say, "No. That's the wrong attitude! I can do everything in Heaven all at once! I need you just as much as you need me. I'm here on your Spirit Team to assist with everything big and small. Call on me for help finding a parking spot, call on me when you feel like you're not hearing messages clearly, call on me when you need validation (even if it's every hour), call on me to help you find the answers and solutions, and I will show up for you each and every time."

Friend, learning to hear, feel, see and know your loved ones' presence can be easier than getting to know your angels because you already know their energy! Think of it like this. You know the vibration of Oneness, God-energy, because you've learned about it in this book and practiced the meditations in the Angel Membership program, right? The energy of Oneness is what angels' energy feels like, but when you connect with your loved ones on the Other Side, there is a human-like energy to them because they've lived a lifetime on Earth.

There is no grounded or rooted energy within angels because they have not had a lifetime here, but there is once you've connected with loved ones. When I was learning energy healing, I created my own method to distinguish who was there, an angel, or loved one. It begins with your thoughts. Let's say you're going about your day and you feel a presence with you. Presence is the first thought. You might think, "Someone is with me right now." Next, ask yourself, "Does this energy feel like Oneness alone or does it feel more Earthly/human?" You will get an immediate sense of the answer. Then go deeper!

If the energy you feel is Oneness alone, an angel is with you. If the energy you feel is Oneness with a grounded, rooted, Earthy energy (or the smell of soil) a loved one is with you. If it is an angel, ask, "Which angel is with me?" You may hear a name, feel a sense of their personality or see the role they play in your life. If the energy is of a departed loved one, ask, "Please allow me to see, hear, feel, and know your personality so I know who is with me." Or ask, "What is your name?"

Your loved ones want to build a stronger connection with you. I was giving one of the first readings of my career when a loved one came through and said to my client, "I need you still, just as much as you need me. I need you to continue our relationship. I need you to remain connected to me." This was new to me at the time so I asked him, "What's the best way for her to stay connected with you?" The ways were countless. As a healer, sometimes the same soul will work with me over a number of years (where their loved ones will book a session a few times a year) and other times departed souls will build off of knowledge another soul gave me in a past session. Over the years, departed souls helped me write this list of ways we can deepen our connection with our loved ones on the Other Side, but always remember the key to each of these is Oneness. Getting into Oneness first will tune you to the energetic radio channel where your loved ones are waiting for you!

ASK YOUR ANGELS FOR HELP

Remember, the angels play different roles in your life. Archangel Sandalphon helps you awaken and connect with the signs/symbols your loved ones in Heaven are using to get your attention. The Cherubs activitate all of the cells within you and molecules surrounding you to make Oneness easier for you to hold. Call on Archangel Chamuel to help you build a relationship with a loved one on the Other Side. Archangel Azrael helps you with the grief process, after we've lost someone we love. Please call on these angels, specifically, and ask them for help when you need it. You can ask them to surround you until your goal is complete and they will honor your request.

SEE DEPARTED LOVED ONES IN DETAIL

After getting into a state of Oneness, the first step in connecting with loved ones in Heaven is to see them in detail. I want you to keep your eyes closed and imagine one loved one in Heaven you wish to connect with. (Side Note: I know that you want to connect with more than one soul, but doing so at the beginning will confuse their energies and you will not learn what I need you to learn, at this moment. For now, it's best to stick with one soul at a time.) Using your imagination, remember every detail of this soul's physical appearance. What do they look like? What is the color of their eyes? What do they smell like? What does it feel like to hold their hand, kiss their cheek, give them a hug? What are they wearing? Do they look like themselves? Younger? I want you to notice all the little details about them.

Concentrating your conscious awareness on the details of your departed loved one is the energetic equivalent of knocking on their front door. It gets their attention. You are calling to their energy and it signals to them that you need them to be present with you at this moment. And that's just what they do! They come to be with you! Then you can go deeper by giving them a hug, and asking them a question.

GIVE YOUR LOVED ONES A HUG

When you see your loved one in your imagination, greet them! Run up to them in your mind and give them a huge bear-hug! Kiss them! Smother them with love and affection! You may see them with tears in their eyes, don't worry! They're just filled with joy to see you! You may hear them whisper something in your ear. They may hand you a gift. They may tell you they've missed you so much, or how proud they are of you, or how much they love you! That's all normal too!

After you've greeted one another, ask your loved one to sit down with you to spend time together. The scenery may change. You may see their home on the Other Side, your home on the Other Side or a place that was familiar to you/them here on Earth (perhaps a home or place you vacationed). Allow the scenery to change in your mind and get comfy, as if you're walking into your living room, sitting on a cozy couch with a cup of tea, ready to chat with someone you love!

ASK YOUR DEPARTED LOVED ONES QUESTIONS

Make Space for Them in Your Life

Once you've sat down with your loved one in your mind, open up to them about where you're at in your life right now. Spill the beans! Tell them everything! What is happening? How are you feeling inside? Where are you stressing or anxious? Where is fear holding you back? What is it that you really want? As you talk with your loved one, questions will naturally arise within you that you want to ask them. The questions you ask may not be about your current life at all. You may ask your loved one to show you where they are in Heaven; what their home looks like; who they are with; what signs they show you; how they validate for you that it's really them! You may ask questions on behalf of another family member. Or you may ask, "What is it that I need to know right now in my life to best serve me on my path?" They will answer each and every question you have to the extent that it does not cross your freewill. They can guide you on a decision, but they cannot choose for you.

If you're asking questions and you feel like you're not getting an answer, try refining the question and asking it in another way (a more detailed way). For example if you ask, "Should I take this new job opportunity and move across the country?" and you don't hear anything back then you need to refine the question. Instead ask, "Would it best serve God's will for my life for me to take this job in California?" Wait for the answer, then ask, "Would it best serve God's will for my life if I stay in the state I currently live in?" You can refine your questions as many times as you'd like until you have the clarity you need.

Sometimes I refine my question over and over and still get "crickets." Silence. When this happens, I ask, "Is it not time for me to know yet?" They'll say "yes," and tell me I don't have all the puzzle pieces I need to make this decision. I'll say, "Will I know in one month? Three months? Six months?" I continue asking this question until I hear a time frame. Sometimes the important thing to do is to live in patience and flow until your angels confirm that it is time for you to receive the answers you're looking for.

CONNECT WITH YOUR LOVED ONES WHILE YOU'RE SLEEPING

Just as we ask to go to the Akashic Records while we rest at night, Spirit says we can also ask God to allow our souls to visit our homes and loved ones in Heaven as we sleep. Some of my clients report back when they try this, and remember their visits with loved ones similar to that of a visitation dream. I've tried this many times and have woken up with a greater sense of peace, but could not recall connecting with my loved ones at night. While I have had visitation dreams before (and I do believe God grants us that ability to connect with our loved ones as we sleep), I've not been able to remember anything. Instead, I tend to wake up feeling my loved ones' presence more palpably and feeling a greater sense of peace. After years of practice, I feel this tool strengthens our ability to connect with our departed loved ones while we are awake. I encourage you to try this, but only with the expectation of feeling more peace and a deeper sense of the presence of your departed loved ones during the day. If you feel a greater magnitude of your loved ones' presence, that's awesome! That means this does work for you!

KEEP THEIR MEMORY ALIVE

Spirit enjoys it when we talk about them, share their memories, or acknowledge their presence. At family functions, some of my clients place a lit candle in front of a framed photo of their loved one. Your loved ones know when you do this and they will mention it in a session! More than the candle or photo, it is your intention that draws their energy to you. You've made space for them to be present with the family as you gather together.

Our loved ones are even with us when we talk about them. In 2019, my family and I took a trip to Marco Island, Florida, and booked a jet ski excursion. Just like my dad instructed me decades ago,

I taught my daughter about the gas and break, how to lean into the turns and jump the waves. She listened enthusiastically and she reminded me of myself as a kid. I told her, "You know I learned all of this from Grandpa Harris. He loved boats, and jet skis, and motorcycles, and anything with an engine! You know he's here with us right now." And I'm certain she felt his presence just as I did.

ACKNOWLEDGE THE SIGNS THEY SHOW YOU

When it comes to your loved ones and signs here's what you need to know. Over time, you'll find that each loved one has a different sign they show you. I know which of my departed loved ones is with me based on the sign I'm receiving:

⌘ My dad will show me: a male cardinal; "Danger Zone" by Kenny Loggins; the movie "Interstellar"; "Don't You Forget About Me" by Simple Minds; "The Living Years" by Mike and The Mechanics (Oh my God—the words of that song are beyond powerful! They make me cry every time. Seriously. Stop right now, and go listen on YouTube while reading the lyrics. They say, "You can listen as well as you hear," and "If you don't give up, you don't give in, you might just be okay." I feel like my dad and I apologize to one another, every time I hear it.). I'll feel his presence out of nowhere as if he's standing next to me, and at times I feel him give me a bear-hug just as I give my daughter a bear-hug.

⌘ My grandma will show me roses, a rosary, or Mother Mary.

⌘ My dad and grandma will come in together sometimes as two cardinals (male and female).

⌘ My Grandpa sends me songs we used to listen to together in the 1990's like "I'll Be Missing You" by Faith Evans and Puff Daddy; "Here With Me" by Dido; and "My Immortal" by Evanescence (the name of which I was having a hard time remembering while typing this and he said, "Go to YouTube search '90's black and white music video female artist'." I was shocked when it just popped up! After that, I went on an errand to Target and there was a large record of this almost twenty-year-old album on display. Grandpa, thank you for helping me write this book)!

The signs your loved one shows you can be the same or different from the signs they show another family member.

One summer, we were in our backyard when I saw a male cardinal. I told my young daughter, "Look! Grandpa's with you!" Her innocent little self was not enthused. "Ugh! If he's coming to visit me, why doesn't he come as a yellow bird? I love yellow birds!" I thought, "Shit! Dad, I've never seen a yellow bird around here. I have no clue how you're going to make that happen!" I told my daughter to ask grandpa for a yellow bird and she did. Low and behold, my dad made it happen! We'd never seen one in the backyard up to that point, but the next week we saw a yellow bird out back every day!

I want you to try this too! You can either assign a loved one a sign you want them to show you or you can allow them to help you identify the signs they're sending you over time. The signs I shared above came to me over a number of years. How did I know? Because that sign made me think of them and feel their presence. Just be aware that your loved ones may like to surprise you with signs they want you to see based on the energy they can control and what's currently happening in your life. What they're trying to say here is not to limit yourself. Be open to all the signs they send to communicate their presence.

KEEP YOUR HEART OPEN

In your auric field, you have a protective shield that is activated by your freewill emotional response. The energy of this shield is like a thick, solid fortress wall that surrounds you in every direction. When you use your freewill to say "no" or "I can't" or "I won't," you activate this shield and in an instant it goes up around you to protect you from whatever it is you fear.

At the beginning, every person who learns to connect with angels or loved ones fears they will not be able to: every single person. Those who succeed, have learned to work through that fear. I say this with complete certainty: the only difference between those who are successful at developing a connection with the Other Side and those who are not is that some quit trying.

Friend, you must keep your heart open. You stay open by praying:

Dear God,

I don't know how you're going to help me build a relationship with my loved ones and angels on the Other Side, but I know you can and I'm here to learn. As long as it takes, I promise to remain open and live in a state of expectancy. In your time not mine, God.

Amen

When you stay open your loved ones don't have to break through a fortress wall-like energy to connect with you. Your openness makes it easier for them! Make gratitude and positive thinking practices to keep your energy field open. When you feel frustrated, count your blessings, your signs, the ways you've grown and what you've learned up until now! You're doing great. Keep going! Keep practicing!

YOU MUST DO THIS TO READ SIGNS

The more you know, the more Spirit can connect with you. You must keep learning until you've got it. Think about how difficult it is to connect with an infant. When they cry, you have no way of truly knowing exactly what they want or what's bothering them. It gets a bit easier with a toddler who can say some words like, "Tummy hurt," and of course it becomes even easier when your kids can talk and read, and you can have full-on conversations with them.

That's what building a relationship with us from the Other Side is like to our loved ones. We all walk through stages growing and building our vocabulary with Spirit. The more we know, the more Spirit can connect with us. I've heard other healers say this and I've seen it for myself with my Angel Reiki School students. Some people who have the gift of medical mediumship can read a book on the human body and start to deliver even deeper messages to their clients than before. Why? Because their vocabulary expanded. Before, Spirit could not show them what the healer did not know. But once they learned it, Spirit could communicate with them on it.

Same goes for you. The more you learn, the more you grow, the bigger your vocabulary gets and the more deeply your loved ones can connect with you. This is why I continue working with spiritual teachers, and only invest in people who are still learning themselves. The more I know, the more I can put together for you. While this book teaches you how to develop a connection with the Other Side for yourself, there is a whole new bag of tools for connecting with Spirit for the purpose of giving readings or doing energy work on others. If this calls to you, the Angel Reiki School will help you develop your spiritual gifts and form a plan for a unique business that utilizes your strengths.

PRACTICE ~~MAKES PERFECT~~ EQUALS SUCCESS

Friend, there is no such thing as perfection but there is success. Building a relationship with your loved ones in Heaven requires your consistency. The more you practice, the better you will become. I recommend making a set appointment time to connect with your loved ones each week. It might be 5–10 minutes a week. You may have 20 minutes to devote or more each week! Awesome! Set an appointment with your loved ones to practice Automatic Writing and stick to it each week.

On Sundays I love taking a bath while connecting with Spirit for the purpose of chatting about my own path. (All the souls I'm connecting with took care of me as a baby and have seen me in my birthday suit so it doesn't faze me). I bring along my pen and notebook, and fully decompress in silence; get into Oneness; unload my burdens from the week; and ask the questions I need answered. I feel my Spirit Team's presence, and channel everything they report onto paper. When I have a rough day, I come back to these writings and they affirm that I'm on the right track, despite whatever is happening at the moment.

WRITE A LETTER TO A LOVED ONE IN HEAVEN

I want you to get into a state of Oneness and practice Automatic Writing with the loved one in Heaven, with whom you had the deepest connection. I want you to write this person a letter. The letter can be as short or as long as you'd like, and you can include whatever comes to you. Write all that flows through you first (until you're not getting any more information), then go back and read what was written. It should be healing and bring peace. Write your letter here:

_____

_____

_____

_____

_____

_____

_____

_____

_____

_____

_____

_____

_____

_____

_____

_____

THROUGH AUTOMATIC WRITING, HAVE THAT SAME LOVED ONE WRITE A LETTER BACK TO YOU

I want you to get into a state of Oneness and practice Automatic Writing with the loved one in Heaven, with whom you had the deepest connection. I want you to get into Oneness and connect with the same loved one you wrote a letter to by seeing them in detail in your imagination. Have them write a letter back to you through Automatic Writing. Ask them what they would like you to know and then write down what comes to you verbatim. Do not try to read/process what is being written as it moves through you to your pen and paper. Instead, write all that flows through you first (until you're not getting any more information), then go back and read what was written. It should be healing. Remember, Spirit only brings through positive, loving messages.

_____

_____

_____

_____

_____

_____

_____

_____

_____

_____

_____

_____

_____

_____

ANGEL
COMMUNICATION
Part 2: Week Three

If you're in the Angel Membership,
go to the Angel Communication Part 2 course
(in the folder titled *A Year With Your Angels*):

☐ Watch **Build Your Spirit Team.**

☐ Watch **Q&A Recording Two**.

BUILD YOUR SPIRIT TEAM

Surrounding you at all times is a group of angels, guides, and loved ones on the Other Side that I call your Spirit Team. Like a physician monitoring your health, or a coach infusing you with self confidence, your Spirit Team is made up of beings sent by God to keep laser focused attention on you. God didn't send you here to suffer. God sent you here to experience all that you are (love, joy, peace, bliss, ease, and grace). God sent you here so that you could be you by listening to your heart. God knew that your presence here would create the change that is needed. God sent you here to enjoy the people, places and things within this world that make you joyful. God knows it's easy to get lost here, that's why They gave you your Spirit Team to function as your reinforcements.

Your Spirit Team is here to ensure that you never get lost: not from God, from your soul-self, your purpose, or your joy. Through your Spirit Team, you always have a connection back to God's energy and back to yourself. Your Spirit Team is here to guide, direct, and protect you without bypassing your freewill. They know every moment of your existence, every past life, every moment coming in this lifetime. Your Spirit Team knows every thought within your head, but they do not judge a single one. They are here to be everything you will ever need.

Over the past three weeks you've worked to better understand which angels and loved ones are with you. Now, it's time to put all that information together so that you know exactly who is on your Spirit Team! In the following pages, you're going to build an overview of your Spirit Team. First, I'm going to have you review your previous angel notes. Then use the following pages to record which angels/ loved ones are working with you and how. This exercise will give you a clear picture of your Spirit Team and how it functions.

When you know who is on your Spirit Team, it simplifies your life just like a team of employees simplifies a business. For example, with my business I need someone to manage the website, someone to answer the phones, someone to edit the podcast and so on. Not just anyone can fill these roles. I don't want a grumpy or negative person answering the phones; I need someone who has an excellent attitude and great customer service. In the same way I don't want someone who doesn't know how to edit podcasts filling this role. I need qualified people who know what they're doing. Friend, the same goes for your Spirit Team.

Through this exercise you'll consolidate your Automatic Writing notes from the past ten weeks and know who is working with you and how. Utilize the strengths of these angels, just like a president distributes responsibilities based on her staff's gifts and natural abilities. You are the president of your team. How does this work? I see myself as using my freewill to work for God. I ask God and my Spirit Team for guidance on all things. I listen to my intuition for the answers. Once I have the answers, I know it is up to me to take action. You must take action in your life, too, and taking action means putting your Spirit Team to work. Once you know your direction, distribute responsibilities by asking specific angels and loved ones to help you based on their strengths.

It's time for you to know exactly who is on your Spirit Team! Review your Automatic Writing notes on each angel, ask the following questions and record what comes through, below:

1. Ask each angel how long they're on your Spirit Team: for your entire life or just for a season?

2. How is each angel currently working with you?

3. What are you working towards with each angel? Did they show you a vision-clip from your future?

4. What sign, symbol, and/or color does each angel show you? After this exercise, you'll have an overview of your Spirit Team, how they're working with you in your everyday life and the signs they send to validate their presence.

EXAMPLE: Archangel Raphael

Archangel Raphael is part of my Spirit Team for my entire life. He has given me a team of healing angels to help others release emotional pain built up within their physical body, and he helps me work on my own health. He shows me I will get my health under control, and I will be healthier from ages 39–105+ than ever before. When he is near I see an outline of him and his team.

Guardian Angel/s

_____

_____

_____

_____

_____

_____

_____

_____

Archangel Michael

_____

_____

_____

_____

_____

_____

_____

_____

_____

Angel Saraphina

_____

_____

_____

_____

_____

_____

_____

_____

_____

_____

Archangel Gabrielle

_____

_____

_____

_____

_____

_____

_____

_____

_____

_____

Archangel Raphael

_____

_____

_____

_____

_____

_____

_____

_____

_____

Archangel Ariel

_____

_____

_____

_____

_____

_____

_____

_____

_____

Archangel Sandalphon

_____

_____

_____

_____

_____

_____

_____

_____

_____

_____

Archangel Raguel

_____

_____

_____

_____

_____

_____

_____

_____

_____

_____

Archangel Raziel

_____

_____

_____

_____

_____

_____

_____

_____

Archangel Haniel

_____

_____

_____

_____

_____

_____

_____

_____

Archangel Chamuel

_____

_____

_____

_____

_____

_____

_____

_____

_____

Archangel Azrael

_____

_____

_____

_____

_____

_____

_____

_____

_____

Archangel Jeremiel

_____

_____

_____

_____

_____

_____

_____

_____

_____

Archangel Uriel

_____

_____

_____

_____

_____

_____

_____

_____

_____

_____

Archangel Jophiel

_____

_____

_____

_____

_____

_____

_____

_____

_____

Archangel Metatron

_____

_____

_____

_____

_____

_____

_____

_____

_____

Archangel Zadkiel

_____

_____

_____

_____

_____

_____

_____

_____

Loved Ones on the Other Side

_____

_____

_____

_____

_____

_____

_____

_____

_____

ANGEL COMMUNICATION
Part 2: Week Four

If you're in the Angel Membership,
go to the Angel Communication Part 2 course
(in the folder titled *A Year With Your Angels*):

☐ Watch **Final Teaching Video.**

BUILDING ANGEL TEAMS

One of the beautiful ways your Spirit Team works is that you can give your burdens, anxieties, negative thoughts, and low vibrational energy to them and they will carry it for you. In fact, you can explore within yourself what weighs you down most and form teams to energetically manage those parts of your life.

For example, I worry constantly about my daughter's well being. With the emergence of Covid, I worried extensively about my husband's health. I have fear about my own health in the future given the heart disease and diabetes that run in my family. I worry about silly little things like having an idea, but no pen or paper to write it down with. In order to keep my Egoic Mind from continually worrying about these big and small things, I've asked God to provide me with teams of angels and loved ones who take and manage these fears for me. I do what I can in every situation here by taking action, and the rest I give to God by surrendering and releasing my lower vibrational energies to my angels. They take this energy and transmute it into love.

I've asked God to provide me with teams of angels in every area of my life including:

1. An angel team to always keep me humbly connected to Oneness and God.
2. An angel team to protect, guide, and uplift my husband.
3. An angel team to continually support and strengthen our marriage.
4. An angel team to keep my daughter safe, joyful, healthy, and well overall in every area of her life.
5. An angel team on my business to ensure I'm always doing my best for those I serve.
6. An angel team around the podcast and this book to ensure it reaches all the people it can benefit.
7. An angel team on my health and well being to keep me healthy and feeling great.
8. An angel team on my joy to ensure that I'm resting and enjoying this life.
9. I assigned an administrative assistant angel to record things if I don't have a pen and paper at the time. He will bring these notes to my mind later on.
10. I have a team of angels who I've asked to support me when taking photos and recording videos, so that I look my best and you can feel Oneness radiating from the photos/videos.

Each one of these teams lifts negative thoughts and worries from my mind and dense energy from my heart so that I don't have to carry burdens/anxieties. As I mentioned earlier, I consider the angel teams I build just as much a part of my team that makes my business work (as my assistant, podcast producer, website designer, etc.) here on Earth.

In the following pages, I'm going to have you work to create teams of angels to carry your fears and anxieties for you. The more honest you are with yourself about what it is you fear or stress about, the more benefit you'll get out of this exercise.

For each of the categories below, write down what things cause you to fear or be anxious. Note how this fear impacts your life. Next, ask God to assign a team of angels to help you specifically in this area of your life. If angels you've worked with previously come to you on a topic (they show you their presence), this means they're working with you on this too, so please record that information below as well. Ask your angels what action steps you can take now, and record what they say. Then allow your angels to lift from your heart any fear or anxiety that remains.

EXAMPLE: Health

> I fear that my family's history of heart disease and diabetes will impact my life. It impacts my life currently in that sometimes I feel paralyzed with fear and thus do not take action on bettering my health. God, please provide me with a team of angels to ensure my highest health in this lifetime. I can see Archangel Raphael and a team of his angels working with me. The action steps they're asking me to take are to eat more whole foods and engage in an activity that makes me sweat for 30 minutes each day.

Your Connection with God, Your Angels and Loved Ones in Heaven

_____

_____

_____

_____

_____

Romantic Relationship

_____

_____

_____

_____

Family

_____

_____

_____

_____

Health

_____

_____

_____

_____

Friends

_____

_____

_____

_____

Career and Work

_____

_____

_____

_____

_____

Money and Finances

_____

_____

_____

_____

_____

Soul's Purpose

_____

_____

_____

_____

_____

Other

_____

_____

_____

_____

_____

BUILDING YOUR EARTHBOUND SPIRIT TEAM

By now, you realize that the work your Spirit Team does to manage your energy, your life, and you is complex. Your angels want you to know that they are always giving you 100%, but that only gets you halfway in life. The other half comes from the work you put in by taking action yourself. When you take action, you're able to go the distance and reach 100% of what you want. Your angels know that living this life isn't easy, and that you need physical comfort and support along the way which is why they encourage you to build a team of people here on Earth who want to support you on your journey. I call this your Earthbound Spirit Team.

My Earthbound Spirit Team is made up of my husband, girlfriends, personal counselor, marriage therapist, chiropractor, intuitive energy healer, financial advisor, myofascial release therapist, babysitter, esthetician, attorney, dentist, my joy list, my hobbies, handyman, my botox lady, and a period tracking app. (Hey, just keeping it real here friends)! This team is a lifeline that keeps my world spinning.

Each person on my Earthbound Spirit Team is like a pillar holding me up. My husband is my home, comfort, safety, and security. My girlfriends bring out my fun side. My personal therapist helps me work through my current life challenges. Self-energy healing, and my chiropractor, energy healer, and myofascial release therapist keep my body's frequency high and energy circulating so it does not become stagnant. My handyman will come over and hang photos that would've otherwise sat for months. My esthetician and botox lady keep me loving my skin. I'm so sensitive to energy I know immediately when the second half of my ovulation cycle starts and my body is pumping estrogen. The period tracking app "Clue" helps me to be more patient with myself at that time and give my body more love.

Any person who is on your Earthbound Spirit Team should want to be there and there should be a reciprocation of energy or payment. I've worked with clients in the past who came back to me after this exercise and said, "Well, I assigned my brother the role of changing my air filter each month, my uncle is a chiropractor so he can do that for free and my dad is an accountant so he can do my taxes." No, friend. It is not healthy to expect others to work for you for free. Your brother needs to be busy at his house changing his own air filter. You are not to build your Earthbound Spirit Team by going around assigning your family and friends jobs they aren't paid for. Your Earthbound Spirit Team lifts you up in your life and is compensated for the work they do in either money or an exchange of services.

Today, I want you to sketch out who you'd like to be on your Earthbound Spirit Team. On the following page is a list of potential people to add to your team. Please circle the ones that resonate with you and add any person/service to this list I may have forgotten.

EARTHBOUND SPIRIT TEAM POSSIBILITIES

It's time for you to build an Earthbound Spirit Team of your own! When we invest in a supportive network of people, our lives become easier, more fun, and more joyful. I view my Earthbound Spirit Team as my Earth Angels. Below is a list of people you may wish to include on your team. As your life changes, this list will change as well. It is not a complete list by any means, so please use the blank spaces to add your own. Circle the team members that most resonate with you then work with them as needed.

Your Joy List	Aromatherapy
Partner or Spouse	Astrologist
Supportive Parents	Attorney
Supportive Siblings	Auto Mechanic
Supportive Friends	Ayurveda
Supportive Family	Babysitters
Personal Counselor	Breathwork
Marriage Therapist	Chakra Balancing
Addiction Counselor	Child Care
Traditional Doctors	Chiropractor
Julie Jancius, The Angel Medium	Craniosacral Therapy
Accountant	Crystal Therapy
Acupuncture	Dentist

Dermatologist

Elder Care

Energy Healer

Esthetician

Faith Leaders

Financial Advisor

Fitness Coach

Food Based Healing

Functional Medicine

Grief Counselor

Home Repair Person

House Cleaner

Insurance Agent

Life Coach

Like-Minded Groups
  (i.e., the Angel Membership)

Massage Therapist

Naturopathy

Neighbors

Nutritionist

Myofascial Release Therapist

Meditation

Mentor

Osteopath

Parent Groups

Period Tracker App (Clue)

Pet Care

Physical Therapist

Pilates

Podcasts

Prayer

Psychiatrist

Qigong

Self Healing

Sound Therapy

Specialist Doctor/s

Spiritual Retreats

Stretching

Support Group

Tai Chi

Yoga

_____

_____

_____

_____

_____

_____

_____

_____

_____

_____

_____

_____

WORKING WITH YOUR ANGELS DAILY

Friend, I'm so proud of you and I hope you're proud of yourself! Over the past twelve weeks, you've done your work to feel God's energy (the energy of your soul), learn to hold Oneness, and get to know your angels. Doesn't it feel great to know who is working with you and how? Now as you move forward here's what you need to know.

When you do not make time for your angels in your life, they will constantly be near you, poking you, trying to get your attention. Have you ever seen a small child try to get their mother's attention while she is talking to another person? The child says, "Mom . . . Mom . . . Mom . . . Mom! Moooommmm!" It's the same energy when it comes to your angels and Spirit Team. If you do not make space for them in your life by having a spiritual practice (a dedicated time to talk to them each week), you will feel like they are constantly poking you and trying to get your attention.

Make time for your angels that fits comfortably into your life. Some people have time to spend 5–10 minutes each day with their angels, others may have 10 minutes on the weekend, others may want to spend more time. You must pray or meditate on the question, "God, how much time should I spend connecting with you and my angels each day or week?" Go with the response that comes to you. It will always be a comfortable time frame for you.

How do you spend time with your angels? For those who are on the go, you may connect mentally with your angels for 10 minutes each day on your lunch break at work. You can ask your angels questions in your mind and see what answers they bring to you. Others may want to sit down, get into a state of Oneness and do some Automatic Writing like you've been doing here the past three months. What your angels want you to know is there is no right or wrong answer. They just want to spend time with you and be a part of your life. They will do this on your terms. The more time and space you give them, the more they will fill it with their presence, support, and love.

This has been a jam-packed crash course introducing you to all of your angels! Teaching you to trust what you hear is a whole other story and box of tools. I hope you'll continue onto my Trust Your Intuition course and then my Find Your Purpose course, as these are the next steps to take in your spiritual awakening journey! In these courses, I teach you how to trust the hearing, seeing, feeling, and knowingness of divine wisdom within you. This is sacred work that takes time to evolve. Be patient with yourself and be proud of how far you've come. You can purchase these courses individually on my website or join my Angel Membership program where you'll have access to these courses within your first year as a member.

Please take a moment to seal the practice and all the work you've done these past few months by spending one more day in Automatic Writing with your angels. Get into Oneness, think back over the past month and ask your angels, "Out of all I've learned, what do you want me to remember most?" Talk to your angels and make a plan for how and when you will connect with them. Then, so that you can see you're capable, ask them any question and record what comes to you.

Friend, I love you! Your Spirit Team, your loved ones in Heaven, and your angels love you so very much! We are all so proud of the amazing work you have done and continue to do in your spiritual training, through this book. Open your heart to all of the unexpected blessings that are coming your way right now, and know that you are worthy of all of them just because you are you! Be courageous, be curious, be inspired, and encouraged!

_____

_____

_____

_____

_____

_____

_____

_____

_____

_____

_____

_____

Acknowledgements

I thank God for allowing me to do Their work every day, and blessing me with this beautiful, magical life. Thank you to my angels for channeling this book through me. This book is dedicated to my angels and yours for their patience in guiding us on our souls' paths.

To my readers, podcast listeners and clients, thank you for being part of my Earthbound Spirit Team. I know any success I have is because of you. Thank you. I consider you my online church congregation that I always dreamt of working with and I cannot thank you enough for entrusting me with your spiritual journey. I pray for you every day and my mission is to provide you with the maximum benefit possible in everything I do.

To my partner, Blake, thank you for teaching me the meaning of unconditional love and for encouraging me to live my joy. I love our love. To the greatest healer I know, my daughter, who I know will go farther in this life than I ever could've dreamed. I love you and am so proud of you. To my dad, Jon Harris, thank you for bringing this gift into my life and teaching me how to build a relationship with you from Heaven. To my mom, Brenda Hawbaker, thank you for building me up with words of faith by always telling me I'd be an author and for teaching me how to dream.

To my college bestie, Sarah Hammer, thank you for being my cheerleader and encouraging all my "crazy" ideas. To my sister, Theresa Schweers, my grandma Donna Scelfo, my aunt, Theresa Scelfo, my cousins and my girls (Kim Russell, Ashley Ballou, and Chef Summer), thank you for being part of my Earthbound Spirit Team, for your love and encouragement—you make this life tons of fun!

To my editor, Sasha Banks, who took my rambling and horrific grammar and made me sound polished—this book wouldn't be what it is without you. To my team for ensuring every angel story is read and every email receives a response, thank you! I deeply appreciate all you do! To my social media volunteer crew, your support gave me the capacity to write this book and I'm so grateful for you.

To Fluff and Lulu, my animal loves, thank you for your warmth, love, and cuddles every time I write.

Thank you to everyone who has been a part of my journey. Any success I have is because of you.

And this book is also dedicated to *you*, beautiful soul. Keep working with your angels. Allow them to help you unfold into the magnificent future that awaits you!

References

Antanaityte, Neringa. (January 1, 2020). *How to Effortlessly Have More Positive Thoughts.* TLEX Institute. https://tlexinstitute.com/how-to-effortlessly-have-more-positive-thoughts/

Bertone, Holly J. (October 27, 2020). *12 Science-Based Benefits of Meditation.* Healthline. https://www.healthline.com/nutrition/12-benefits-of-meditation#1.-Reduces-stress

Carr, Sam. (February 21, 2021). *How Many Ads Do We See A Day in 2021?.* PPC Protect. https://ppcprotect.com/how-many-ads-do-we-see-a-day/

English, Trevor. (February 28, 2020). *You Are Mostly Made Up of Empty Space.* Interesting Engineering. https://interestingengineering.com/due-to-the-space-inside-atoms

Hopler, Whitney. (July 19, 2018). *Who Are Cherubim Angels?.* Learn Religions. https://www.learnreligions.com/what-are-cherubim-angels-123903

Kornfield, Jack. (June 6, 2000). *After the Ecstasy, the Laundry: How the Heart Grows Wise on the Spiritual Path.* Bantam.

Kurichenko, Victoria. (October 8, 2020). *67 Positive Daily Affirmations to Become Your Better Self.* Medium. https://medium.com/live-your-life-on-purpose/67-positive-daily-affirmations

Join Julie's

ANGEL MEMBERSHIP PROGRAM

"It's like having a session with Julie each week!"

Julie's Angel Membership program walks you through the steps of spiritual growth while allowing your Angels and Spirit Team to support your journey.

When you sign up, you'll have access to:

- ⌘ Julie's *A Year With Your Angels Program* including twelve courses (one month at a time).
- ⌘ Dozens of Julie's prerecorded meditations and guided energy healing sessions.
- ⌘ Small groups led by Julie.
- ⌘ Live group meetings / sacred events with Julie each month where you can ask her questions.
- ⌘ A private online community where you can connect with hundreds of like-minded souls who are awakening too.
- ⌘ And so much more!

Join us today to begin learning the power of the divine within you!
Register online at: www.theangelmedium.com

WWW.THEANGELMEDIUM.COM

Julie Jancius'

ANGEL REIKI SCHOOL

Develop your unique spiritual gifts, learn energy healing and become an Angel Reiki Master Teacher.

Do you feel called to be a healer?

Are you ready to develop your God-given spiritual gifts?

Maybe you're an empath who is ready to
STOP taking on other people's energy . . .

If you answered "YES" to any of those things,
the Angel Reiki School is what you've been waiting for . . .
it will teach you all of these life-changing skills and more!

Visit my www.theangelmedium.com to get started today!

WWW.THEANGELMEDIUM.COM

SPECIAL GIFT FOR YOU

Hello, Beautiful Soul!

Thank you so much for purchasing this book.

As a special gift to you, please visit my website www.theangelmedium.com and click on the menu tab "Book." There you can register for access to tons of awesome freebies to help you on your spiritual journey!

Sending you peace, bliss and many blessings,

Julie and Your Angels

WWW.THEANGELMEDIUM.COM

ABOUT THE AUTHOR
JULIE JANCIUS

Julie Jancius is The Angel Medium™ and host of "Angels and Awakening," rated one of the country's Top 10 spiritual podcasts, receiving 1.3+ million downloads a year in 70+ countries around the world.

She is the founder of Angel Reiki Energy Healing, and is a world-renowned angel expert on a mission to teach others how to connect with their angels and loved ones on the Other Side in order to make this life "Heaven on Earth."

In 2015, Julie thought she was going crazy when she suddenly began hearing her intuition clearly and seeing visions. To her shock and surprise, her estranged father had passed away on the same day she started seeing visions—her dad had been communicating with her from the Other Side, the entire time! To understand how this was happening, Julie left her corporate career to study with world-renowned, God-based healers. Each time she works with a client, their Spirit Team (angels, guides and loved ones) is right there waiting to deliver positive, uplifting messages. Her life's work is about teaching others how to make that connection for themselves.

In *Angels and Awakening,* Julie expertly breaks down complex spiritual topics, making them easy to incorporate into everyday life. Through her inspirational talks, books, podcast, courses, and possible upcoming TV show, Julie will help you understand who you truly are, your soul's purpose, and how to deepen your connection with the Other Side.

For more info or to join the Angel Reiki School with Julie Jancius visit:
www.theangelmedium.com
Instagram.com/angelpodcast/
Facebook.com/groups/angelpodcast
TikTok: @angelpodcast

—

Made in the USA
Las Vegas, NV
20 November 2021